D1093583

THE OCCASIONAL PAPERS
OF
MR. JUSTICE BURTON

Burton, H. H.

The Occasional Papers of Mr. Justice Burton

EDWARD G. HUDON, *Editor*

BOWDOIN COLLEGE
Brunswick, Maine

1969

Copyright 1969 by The President and Trustees of Bowdoin College

Library of Congress Catalog Number: 74-76778

Printed by The Anthoensen Press, Portland, Maine

340
B974a   169378

Foreword

FEW MEN have been more closely associated with Bowdoin College throughout their lives than Harold Hitz Burton of the Class of 1909, Associate Justice of the Supreme Court of the United States from 1945 until he retired in 1958 to continuing but less strenuous service on the United States Court of Appeals for the District of Columbia.

Few men, in their careers, have more fully heeded the admonition of President McKeen in his address when the College first opened its doors to students:

> It ought always to be remembered that literary institutions are founded and endowed for the common good, and not for the private advantage of those who resort to them. It is not that they may be able to pass through life in an easy or reputable manner, but that their mental powers may be cultivated and improved for the benefit of society.

In 1937 when Harold Burton was Mayor of Cleveland the College bestowed on him the degree of Doctor of Laws. President Sills in his citation presented him as representing those "who have given freely of themselves to the public service." He was again honored by his College when in 1958 he was awarded "The Bowdoin Prize." This award is given once in five years to that member of the College "who shall have made during the period the

[v]

Mills College Library
MWithdraweGE
LIBRARY

most distinctive contribution in any one field of human endeavor."

During his years of service on the Court, Mr. Justice Burton severely limited his other activities. He accepted few speaking engagements. He did, however, regularly address the Judicial Conference of the Third Circuit, his own circuit, and occasionally in the period between sessions of the Court spoke before other legal gatherings, traditionally relating his remarks to the history and heritage of our highest court.

It is a privilege for the College to join with Mrs. Harold H. Burton in making these occasional papers available.

JAMES STACY COLES
President of Bowdoin College

August, 1967

ACKNOWLEDGMENTS

THE "occasional papers" included in this volume were for the most part originally given as addresses and then were subsequently published. The facts about each are listed below:

"Judging Is Also Administration": An Appreciation of Constructive Leadership.

Address before the Section of Judicial Administration, American Bar Association, Cleveland, Ohio, September 24, 1947.
Published in 33 American Bar Association Journal 1099 (November, 1947).

The Cornerstone of Constitutional Law: The Extraordinary Case of *Marbury* v. *Madison*.

Address at the Judicial Conference of the Third Judicial Circuit of the United States, Atlantic City, New Jersey, July 18, 1950.
Published in 36 American Bar Association Journal 805 (October, 1950).

"Justice the Guardian of Liberty": John Marshall at the Trial of Aaron Burr.

Address at the Judicial Conference of the Third Judicial Circuit of the United States, Atlantic City, New Jersey, July 17, 1951.
Published in 37 American Bar Association Journal 735 (October, 1951).

The Story of the Place: Where First and A Streets Formerly Met at What Is Now the Site of the Supreme Court Building.

Published in 21 The George Washington Law Review 253 (January, 1953).

The Dartmouth College Case: A Dramatization.

Address at the Judicial Conferences of the Third and Tenth Judicial Circuits of the United States, Atlantic City, New Jersey, July 9, 1952, and Denver, Colorado, July 18, 1952.
Published in 38 American Bar Association Journal 991 (December, 1952).

An Independent Judiciary: The Keystone of Our Freedom.

Address at the Judicial Conference of the Third Judicial District, Atlantic City, New Jersey, July 7, 1963.
Published in 39 American Bar Association Journal 1067 (December, 1953).

Two Significant Decisions: *Ex parte Milligan* and *Ex parte McCardle*.

Address to the Iota Theta Law Fraternity, New York, New York,

September 22, 1954, and to the Student Legal Forum at the University of Virginia Law School, Charlottesville, Virginia, September 30, 1954. Published in 41 American Bar Association Journal 121 (February, 1955).

John Marshall: The Man.

Published in 104 University of Pennsylvania Law Review 3 (October, 1955).

The *Legal Tender* Cases: A Celebrated Supreme Court Reversal.

Published in 42 American Bar Association Journal 231 (March, 1956).

The Independence and Continuity of the Supreme Court of the United States.

Address at the National Convention of the Phi Alpha Delta Law Fraternity, Cleveland, Ohio, June 22, 1956.

The American Bar Association Journal, The George Washington Law Review, and the University of Pennsylvania Law Review have consented to the inclusion of the papers originally published by them, and their copyrights are noted.

The assistance of Thomas E. Waggaman, formerly Marshal of the Supreme Court of the United States who cooperated with Mr. Justice Burton in writing "The Story of the Place," and of Edward G. Hudon, formerly of the United States Supreme Court Library and now in the United States District Attorney's Office for Maine, has been of great value.

The secretarial staff of the Bowdoin College President's Office, Miss Kathryn Drusilla Fielding and Mrs. Lucille Sinnett, has given invaluable assistance, as have the College Editor, Edward Born, and his Assistant, Miss Edith E. Lyon.

Contents

Introduction

HAROLD HITZ BURTON was born in Jamaica Plain, Massachusetts, June 22, 1888. On his father's side his family
had roots in Maine reaching back almost two centuries. His
father, Alfred E. Burton, a civil engineer, Bowdoin faculty
member, and the first Dean of Massachusetts Institute of
Technology, was born in Portland. On his mother's side his
great-grandfather, John Hitz, was the first Swiss Consul
General to the United States. Prophetically, the Hitz home
in Washington stood diagonally across the street from the
site of the present Supreme Court building.

Harold Burton's early education was in Switzerland where
his mother had returned for her health. After her death he
returned to the United States. He graduated from the New-
ton, Massachusetts, High School and in the fall of 1905
entered Bowdoin College. He graduated *summa cum laude*
in the Class of 1909. Few have had a brighter undergraduate
record, and few have had a closer lifetime association with
the College. A quarterback, a track man, editor-in-chief of
the *Bugle*, and member of Delta Kappa Epsilon and Phi Beta
Kappa, he contributed importantly to all aspects of college
life. Son of a Bowdoin father who served the College as an
Overseer, he was himself the father of two Bowdoin men
and grandfather of another; he served successively as a member of the Alumni Council, as a Director of the Alumni
Fund, and as an Overseer of the College. Like many another,
he made the short trip from Brunswick to Cambridge and
there received his Bachelor of Laws degree from Harvard
in 1912.

A lawyer who served important clients in Utah, Idaho,
and Ohio, a captain of infantry in World War I, decorated
by two governments, a layman whose contributions to his
church were uniquely recognized during his service as na-

tional moderator of the American Unitarian Association—
there is much one could say of him. One thing, however,
was preeminent: his dedication to the common good. A long-
time associate wrote: "His was a career distinguished by almost every imaginable form of public service, rendered with
great modesty, unflinching courage, and the highest ideals."

In a governmental system, one of whose essential features
is the separation of powers, Harold Burton achieved distinction in all three branches—the executive, the legislative, and
the judicial. He entered public service when he accepted
that vital but thankless assignment—membership on a local
school board, in this case that of East Cleveland. In the same
year he was elected a member of the Ohio House of Representatives. He served for more than two years as director of
law for the City of Cleveland. It was as mayor of Cleveland
that he first won national attention. "The good people of
Cleveland showed their gratitude," a commentator has written, "by sending back for a total of three terms the man who
returned good government to them in troublesome, messy,
depression times."

The people of Ohio liked what he did for their largest city.
In 1940 they elected him to the United States Senate. There
he was known as one who was present at roll calls, read and
answered as much of his own mail as he could, arrived early
at work, and individually prepared himself on the issues he
had to debate. He was one of the authors of the Ball-Burton-
Hatch-Hill Resolution (popularly known as B_2H_2), calling
for American support of international cooperation at a time
when senatorial opposition to the League of Nations was
much in men's minds. He co-sponsored the Hill-Burton Hos-
pital Construction Act which gave an impetus to the building of hospitals throughout the country. He supported Lend-
Lease, and the reciprocal trade agreement program. He
favored cloture in the poll tax debate. He was best known,
however, as an influential member of Senator Truman's

Committee to investigate the National Defense Program during World War II. His work in it was so valuable, it has been said, that had he not been a Republican, he would have been chosen chairman when Mr. Truman resigned to become Vice President.

In 1945 his former committee chairman, now President of the United States, and in a totally nonpartisan act, appointed him Associate Justice of the Supreme Court of the United States. His record in the thirteen terms of court in which he served deepened his reputation for hard work, integrity, moderation, and a dedication to the common good. He once told a dignified judicial gathering that he thought the role of the Supreme Court in the American governmental system was well stated by the small boy who said: "Well, when we want to last a full nine-inning game, then we have an umpire." In one of his first opinions—a dissent, by the way—he said:

> The courts, as well as our other agencies of the Government, accordingly owe a constitutional obligation not to invade the fields reserved either to the people, the States, or the other coordinate branches of the Government. (327 U.S. 304, 338)

He joined five of his brethren to tell the President that he had exceeded his constitutional powers; he was a member of the unanimous court that told the states that in the exercise of their own power to establish school systems they must stay within the limits of the Fourteenth Amendment; he did not hesitate to differ with his colleagues when he thought they were dangerously restricting the freedom of action of the executive in time of war; and he spoke for the Court in finding a fair trial absent when a confidential informant's identity was withheld. At all times he adhered resolutely to his concept of the role of the Court as umpire. He called them as he saw them.

Mr. Justice Burton was deeply interested in the institution of which he was a part; in its history and traditions. Out of that interest came the occasional papers, reprinted here.

ATHERN PARK DAGGETT

William Nelson Cromwell Professor of Constitutional and International Law and Government—Bowdoin College

THE OCCASIONAL PAPERS
OF
MR. JUSTICE BURTON

I

"Judging Is Also Administration"

AN APPRECIATION OF CONSTRUCTIVE LEADERSHIP*

ON JUNE 30, 1921, former President William Howard Taft was nominated Chief Justice of the United States. At the October Term he found the Supreme Court of the United States more than a year behind in its docket.[1] The Court was flooded not only with cases entitled to full consideration but with many not justifying further review. The Court sat in the much-liked original Senate Chamber in the Capitol but lacked adequate facilities for its library, its Clerk, its Marshal, the members of its Bar, and the chambers of its Justices. The rules of procedure throughout the federal court system were antiquated and cumbersome. Many of the lower federal courts were behind in their dockets, but there was little authoritative information by which to measure the need for additional permanent district or circuit judges. There was no coordination between the administrative offices of the federal courts, much less any businesslike control over their operations. There was no authorized procedure for mobilizing the experience of the courts to help Congress consider legislation dealing with judicial administration. Instead of translating the tremendous motive power of the people into efficient judicial action, the administration of our courts often handicapped the judges in dispensing justice. It was clear that not only wisdom and clarity but also speed and efficiency were essential to the judicial process. "Judging is also administration";[2] and in the face of such conditions, Chief Justice Taft and his successors in office have demonstrated the value of competent judicial administration to the cause of justice.

* Reprinted by permission of the American Bar Association Journal.

Almost exactly twenty years later, when Chief Justice Charles Evans Hughes, on July 1, 1941, retired from his eleven years of arduous service which followed the equally arduous nine of his predecessor, the judicial administration of the Supreme Court of the United States had changed from a cause of national concern to one of national pride. The federal judiciary had been converted from an outstanding example of an unordered judiciary to an outstanding example of efficient judicial administration. Chief Justices Harlan Fiske Stone and Fred M. Vinson have maintained this high standard.

The period 1921-1941 was a time when economic readjustments led to many fundamental changes in governmental structures and policies. Nevertheless, through the application of the wide executive experience of the two Chief Justices of the United States who served in that period, the courts of the United States not only preserved our judicial structure but also strengthened it.

The technique of the judicial process is as properly the responsibility of the judges and lawyers as the technique of automobile production is the responsibility of mechanical, industrial, and financial experts. Judicial administration is largely a technical matter dealing with the jurisdiction, structure, procedure, personnel, and equipment of the courts and of their administrative agencies. Each of these subjects in our federal judicial system needed and received the personal attention of Chief Justices Taft and Hughes. They came to this task of judicial administration equipped with an extraordinary wealth of appropriate experience. In addition to several years of federal judicial experience, each had had long and practical experience in dealing with the executive and legislative procedure of a free and representative government. Each had an appreciation of the initiative, determination, and patience required to secure the substantial improvements sought.[3] Chief Justice Taft laid the essential foundations for the improved judicial administration of the federal courts. Chief Justice Hughes built important super-structures upon those foundations.

Of their contributions to the improvement of judicial administration five are emphasized here:

1. The Coordination of the Federal Judiciary.

2. The Enlargement of the Discretionary, and the Restriction of the Obligatory, Jurisdiction of the Supreme Court.

3. The Building and Equipment of the Supreme Court Building.

4. The Federal Rules of Civil Procedure.

5. The Administrative Office of the United States Courts.

1. *The Coordination of the Federal Judiciary*

Traditionally, not only the Supreme Court, but also each court of the United States had been administratively independent of every other court and of every administrative control. While litigated cases moved from court to court, and orders issued by the several courts generally were obeyed by those to whom they were directed, there was little coordination of administrative service. There was no statistical information, authoritatively analyzed, as to the work of the courts. Statistical material presented to Congress as a basis for appropriations was collected largely by the Attorney General of the United States. This produced the inappropriate result that the federal courts, before which the Attorney General's staff constantly appeared, were dependent upon that same Attorney General for recommendations in support of appropriations for the courts.

In 1921, the most pressing need of the federal courts was for additional judges or for a reduction in pending cases. The absence of factual data as to the comparative needs of the different districts made it difficult for anyone to determine what relief might be secured by temporary reassignments of judges between districts and even between circuits. Furthermore, there was no judicial authority adequate to make such reassignments or even to bring judges together to prepare recommendations as to the relative needs of their respective districts.

As soon as William Howard Taft became Chief Justice, he brought to bear on this issue his unique combination of experience as a Circuit Judge and as President of the United States. He saw all sides of the question. As President he had devoted much attention to the appointments he made to the federal judiciary and he had approved the creation of two new courts, namely, the United States Court of Customs Appeals[4] and the United States Commerce Court.[5] Since 1909, the American Bar Association had advocated judicial reform pointing toward a unified judiciary and a judicial council.[6] In 1914, after leaving the Presidency, Mr. Taft had urged the establishment of a council of federal judges "to consider each year the pending Federal judicial business of the country and to distribute [the] Federal judicial force of the country through the various districts and intermediate appellate courts, so that the existing arrears may be attacked and disposed of."[7]

As Chief Justice, he gave his vigorous support[8] to a proposed amendment to the Judicial Code providing for the summoning annually by the Chief Justice of the United States of a Conference of the Senior Circuit Judges to meet in Washington on the last Monday in September. The amendment proposed, among other things, that—

> Said conference shall make a comprehensive survey of the condition of business in the courts of the United States and prepare plans for assignment and transfer of judges to or from circuits or districts where the state of the docket or condition of business indicates the need therefor, and shall submit such suggestions to the various courts as may seem in the interest of uniformity and expedition of business.[9]

The bill also authorized a senior circuit judge to reassign district judges of his circuit temporarily to where they might be most needed in that circuit. Under certain limitations, the Chief Justice of the United States, likewise, was authorized to assign to such duty a district judge or a circuit judge from outside the circuit where the need existed.[10] He said of this proposal:

> These provisions allow team work. They throw upon the council of judges, which is to meet annually, the responsibility of making the judicial force in the courts of first instance as effective as may be. They make possible the executive application of an available force to do a work which is distributed unevenly throughout the entire country. It ends the absurd condition, which has heretofore prevailed, under which each district judge has had to paddle his own canoe and has done as much business as he thought proper.[11]

As finally adopted, September 14, 1922, the act also authorized the appointment of twenty-four additional district judges.[12]

This application of administrative common sense to an uncoordinated judicial system provided a permanent mechanism for securing factual appraisals of the requirements of the respective districts for adjustments in judicial manpower. It established a natural agency for the coordination of policies and for the consideration, and even initiation, of legislative proposals affecting the judiciary. For example, the regular session of this Conference, held October 1-4, 1946, dealt with twenty-two administrative and legislative problems none of which otherwise could have received comparable attention and as to which the executive and legislative branches of the Government otherwise could not have received as competent an opinion.[13]

[7]

2. The Enlargement of the Discretionary, and the Restriction of the Obligatory, Jurisdiction of the Supreme Court

In 1924, except upon an order for advancement, it still required a year to reach a case on the Docket of the Supreme Court.[14] In the years immediately preceding the October Term, 1925, the obligatory jurisdiction of the Court accounted for over 80 percent of the cases on its appellate docket, or about 250 cases a year. The remaining 20 percent consisted of sixty to seventy cases in which petitions for certiorari had been granted, out of about 500 such petitions directed to the discretionary jurisdiction of the Court.[15] As long as the obligatory jurisdiction thus applied to so much of the docket, there was little hope of limiting hearings to cases of public significance or of relieving the Court from hearing cases which presented no substantial reason for a further review. With an approaching increase of federal litigation, the Court foresaw that its docket would be so filled with cases under its obligatory jurisdiction that it would not be able to give to issues of public concern the attention they deserved. On the other hand, the establishment of the Circuit Courts of Appeals,[16] and the abolition of the Circuit Courts,[17] together with the authorization of a partially discretionary control by the Supreme Court over the cases to be reviewed from those courts,[18] were providing a satisfactory solution within the limited class of cases thus affected. The mechanism controlling this discretionary jurisdiction was proving to be one of the best devices for governmental control of discretionary procedure in this nation's broad experience with checks and balances.

Thus fortified by thirty years of experience with petitions for certiorari, the Court, even before Chief Justice Taft joined it, had appointed a Committee of Justices to prepare legislation which would further restrict the obligatory jurisdiction of the Court and would substitute for it the Court's discretionary jurisdiction.[19] The bill became known as the Judges' Bill and the plan proposed by the Justices was to limit reviews much more strictly to cases in which a petition for certiorari had been granted. Due largely to the active sponsorship of it by the Chief Justice and the Court's Committee of Justices, it was approved February 13, 1925.[20] It has been eminently successful and has become the basic mechanism in maintaining a flexible, but firm, control over the volume of the Supreme Court's work.

The granting or denial of a petition for certiorari is not a decision on the merits of the case. Nearly every case in which a petition for certiorari is required has been heard previously by a federal or state court of three or more judges. In most of them, a separate trial court also has passed upon the issues. The character of the reasons guiding the Supreme Court's discretion in acting on petitions for certiorari are stated in its rules.[21] Accordingly, nearly all of the cases decided in the Circuit Courts of Appeals no longer are reviewable in the Supreme Court except upon a writ of certiorari, which is granted only in the discretion of the Supreme Court. This has enabled the Supreme Court to protect itself against such abuse of its jurisdiction by litigants as previously had occurred and again was being threatened. The danger of an overloaded docket, without such a check, is evident from the fact that, from 1925 to the present, the denial of these petitions at each Term has averaged about 80 percent of those filed.[22] Without further explanation, such a high percentage might suggest a possible abuse of its own discretion, by the Court, in unduly restricting access to it. However, a unique practice of the Court, fully explained to Congress, has provided an excellent safeguard against such a possibility. This safeguard is the practice of the Court to grant any such petition upon the favorable vote of a substantial minority—that is, four out of nine—of the members of the Court rather than to require the favorable vote of a majority. Unless at least a substantial minority of the Court believes that the case should be heard, it seems clear that it should not be. On the other hand, if a substantial minority of the members of the Court feels that it should be heard, the Court, as a whole, hears it and passes upon the issue it presents.[23]

The Act of 1925 had the hoped-for results. From the time its full effect was felt, the Court has been current with its business. At the close of the October Term, 1929, which was presided over in turn by Chief Justice Taft, Mr. Justice Holmes and Chief Justice Hughes, the Court made the official entry that it had disposed of all cases submitted to it and all business before the Court at that Term.[24] Of its October Term, 1930, it has been stated that "on any basis of comparison the Court cleared its docket more than at any time during the last hundred years."[25] Of its October Term, 1932, it is said:

> In effect, for the first time since the early years of its institution, the Court is hearing and disposing of all litigation brought before it without delay and without sacrifice of any of the guarantees of ample argument and due deliberation which the effective exercise of its functions demand. In so doing, it sets a standard for state courts of last resort throughout the country.[26]

That act was born of judicial experience. It was written into law and put into operation under the leadership of Chief Justice Taft. The high standards of judicial administration which it made possible have been maintained to this day.

3. *The Building and Equipment of the Supreme Court Building*

From its earliest days, the Supreme Court, its library and its staff were handicapped by lack of adequate space and facilities. A "building for the Judiciary" was among the recommendations of a Committee of the House of Representatives in 1796 and the original plans for the Capitol included no room for the Court. However, for about 135 years, no "building for the Judiciary" was built and, during that time, the Court was housed in space temporarily assigned to it in the Capitol. During its first eight years, the Court met in a small room, 24 feet wide by 30 feet long, which was then known as the Senate Clerk's office. Later, during most of Chief Justice Marshall's service, the Court met in a room in the basement beneath the then Senate Chamber. The space for its library and its Clerk was inadequate and the Justices maintained their chambers in their respective homes. In 1860, when the Senate moved into its new Wing of the Capitol, the Court was moved upstairs to the original Senate Chamber.[27] This provided a hearing room to which the Court became greatly attached. Its former courtroom was used for a law library. However, as time went on, the increasing business of the Court far outgrew the space allotted to its Clerk, its Marshal, its Justices and the members of its Bar.

Again Chief Justice Taft took the lead. This time he induced Congress to see the appropriateness of providing the Supreme Court with facilities comparable to those of the legislative and executive branches of the Government and reasonably adapted to the needs of the future. The purchase of a site opposite the Capitol was authorized in 1926.[28] The United States Supreme Court Building Commission was created in 1928.[29] Chief Justice Hughes, succeeding Chief Justice Taft as Chairman of the Building Commission, was able not only to secure completion of the building in time to use it throughout the October Term, 1935, but to do so for less than the sum appropriated.[30]

Today not only does the simple majesty of the Supreme Court Building inspire the members of the Court and the public, but its facilities have increased the efficiency of the

[11]

Court. The building houses not only the courtroom, the law library, the Clerk's office and the Marshal's office, but also the Justices' chambers, the Justices' library, conference rooms for the Judicial Conference of Senior Circuit Court Judges and other appropriate bodies, rooms for the Attorney General, the Solicitor General and members of the Bar, rooms for the Court Reporter and his staff, a print shop for the printing of opinions, the Administrative Office of the United States Courts, and a cafeteria for the visiting public as well as the employees. As a result, the Court has substantially adequate physical facilities and seeks to render services worthy of them.

4. *The Federal Rules of Civil Procedure*

Having thus put its own house in order, the Supreme Court, under the leadership of Chief Justice Hughes and of the Judicial Conference of Senior Circuit Judges, undertook to meet the long-felt need for generally simplified federal court procedure. In 1914, seven years before William Howard Taft became Chief Justice, he had coupled his advocacy of simplified procedure with his advocacy of a Judicial Conference.[31] Chief Justice Hughes had a like interest in this subject. With the support of the American Bar Association, legislation was secured which authorized the Supreme Court "to prescribe, by general rules, for the district courts of the United States and for the courts of the District of Columbia, the forms of process, writs, pleadings, and motions, and the practice and procedure in civil actions at law." It expressly provided also that "The court may at any time unite the general rules prescribed by it for cases in equity with those in actions at law so as to secure one form of civil action and procedure for both: . . . ."[32] Under this authority, an outstanding Advisory Committee was appointed by the Supreme Court.[33] Its service was competent and diligent. Through several publications of its preliminary drafts and comments, it forestalled as many errors and ambiguities as it could. Following the Committee's Final Report, the Supreme Court adopted the new Federal Rules of Civil Procedure December 20, 1937, and these became effective September 16, 1938.[34] This procedure led to similar action which produced the new Federal Rules of Criminal Procedure, effective March 21, 1946.[35]

5. *The Administrative Office of the United States Courts*

There still remained to be taken the unprecedented but essential step of providing the federal courts with a business administration of their affairs without undue interference with their independence.

Without the Judicial Conference of Senior Circuit Judges and the coordination of the administration of the federal courts resulting from it, this step would have been inconceivable. However, when the members of the Conference became convinced of the desirability of a coordinated federal judiciary, the Administrative Office of the United States Courts was but a natural implementation of the idea.

By the Act of August 7, 1939, Congress gave the necessary authority.[36] The Supreme Court appointed Henry P. Chandler Director and Elmore Whitehurst Assistant Director.[37] The Administrative Office has proved its value many times over—not only to the Chief Justice of the United States, the Supreme Court and the Judicial Conference of Senior Circuit Judges but also to the Circuit Courts of Appeals, the District Courts, the Special Courts, the Department of Justice and to Congress. For the first time, authoritative judicial statistics are available, supervision is given to every financial responsibility of the federal courts, efficiency is gained in securing quarters and equipment, technical assistance is available for the supervision of developments in administrative activities such as those of official reporters, bankruptcy referees, U. S. Commissioners and probation officers. The Administrative

Office is now an integral part of the federal judicial system and it has a flexibility that will permit it to meet the demands of the future.

As a result of the constructive leadership in judicial administration that has been described, our federal courts today are coordinated, the Supreme Court Docket is current, the Supreme Court is adequately housed and equipped, simplified Federal Rules of Civil and Criminal Procedure are in effect and a permanent Administrative Office for the Courts of the United States is in operation.

The eyes of the world watch each test of the constitutional structure of the United States. The keystone of that structure is its independent judiciary. It remains for that judiciary to fit its actions so perfectly to the needs of each opportunity that they will strengthen the case for a government of laws as the best guaranty of human liberty.

NOTES TO CHAPTER I

1. "By 1921 it required between something more than a year to something less than two years for a case to be reached for argument after its docketing, and there was grave ground for apprehension that the calendar would soon become even more congested." Charles E. Hughes, Jr., in Proceedings in Memory of Mr. Justice Van Devanter, 316 U. S. V, XII.

On March 30, 1922, Chief Justice Taft estimated that it then took eighteen to twenty-four months to reach an ordinary case on the docket. Hearing before Committee on the Judiciary, House of Representatives, on H. R. 10479, 67th Cong., 2d Sess. 7, 12.

2. Hart, The Business of the Supreme Court at the October Terms, 1937 and 1938, 53 Harv. L. Rev. 579, 613. That article is the concluding one in the following series covering the Judicial Administration of the Supreme Court of the United States since 1789:

Frankfurter and Landis, The Business of the Supreme Court (1789-O. T. 1926); Frankfurter and Landis, The Supreme Court under the Judiciary Act of 1925 (O. T. 1927), 42 Harv. L. Rev. 1; Frankfurter and Landis, The Business of the Supreme Court at October Term, 1928, 43 id. 33; (O. T. 1929), 44 id. 1; (O. T. 1930), 45 id. 271; (O. T. 1931), 46 id. 226; Frankfurter and Hart (O. T. 1932), 47 id. 245; (O. T. 1933), 48 id. 238; (O. T. 1934), 49 id. 68; Frankfurter and Fisher (O. T. 1935 and 1936), 51 id. 577.

3. Chief Justice Taft, in addition to many years spent in the general practice of his profession, in professional organizations, and in his service

as Chief Justice of the United States, 1921-1930, served as: Assistant Prosecuting Attorney of Hamilton County, Ohio, 1881-1883; Assistant County Solicitor of Hamilton County, 1885-1887; Judge of the Superior Court in Cincinnati, Ohio, 1887-1890; Solicitor General of the United States, 1890-1892; U. S. Circuit Judge for the Sixth Circuit, 1892-1900; Professor and Dean of the Law Department, University of Cincinnati, 1896-1900; President of the U. S. Philippine Commission, and later the First Civil Governor of the Philippine Islands, 1900-1904; Secretary of War, 1904-1908; and President of the United States, 1909-1913. During his Presidency, Congress adopted the Judicial Code of March 3, 1911, and he appointed to the Supreme Court Associate Justices Lurton, Hughes, Van Devanter, J. R. Lamar and Pitney. He also appointed Associate Justice White as Chief Justice of the United States. From 1913 to 1921 he served as Kent Professor of Law at Yale University.

Chief Justice Hughes, in addition to his general practice of his profession, his activity in professional organizations and his service as Chief Justice of the United States, 1930-1941, served as: Professor of Law and Lecturer at Cornell and at the New York School of Law, 1891-1900; counsel for the Stevens Gas Commission (N. Y. Legislature), 1905; counsel for the Armstrong Insurance Commission (N. Y. Legislature), 1905-1906; Governor of New York, 1907-1910; Associate Justice of the Supreme Court of the United States, 1910-1916; Candidate for President of the United States, 1916; Secretary of State of the United States, 1921-1925; member of the Permanent Court of Arbitration, The Hague, 1926-1930; Judge of the Permanent Court of International Justice, 1928-1930.

4. Act of August 5, 1909, 36 Stat. 105. It is now the United States Court of Customs and Patent Appeals, Act of March 2, 1929, 45 Stat. 1475.

5. Act of June 18, 1910, 36 Stat. 539. Abolished by Act of October 22, 1913, 38 Stat. 219.

6. Report of the Special Committee to Suggest Remedies and Formulate Proposed Laws to Prevent Delay and Unnecessary Cost in Litigation, 34 Am. Bar Assn. Rep. 578.

7. William H. Taft, The Attacks on the Courts and Legal Procedure, Address at Cincinnati Law School Commencement, May 23, 1914, 5 Ky. L. J. 1, 15.

8. His support included, among other efforts, his testimony of October 5, 1921, in the Hearings on S. 2432, 2433 and 2523, before the Senate Committee on the Judiciary, 67th Cong., 1st Sess. 11. During the pendency of the Bill in Congress, he spoke on this subject before the American Bar Association at Cincinnati, August 10, 1921, 46 Am. Bar Assn. Rep. 561, and at San Francisco, August 10, 1922, 8 Am. Bar Assn. J. 601, 47 Am. Bar Assn. Rep. 250, 6 J. Am. Jud. Soc. 36, 57 Am. L. Rev. 1 and the Chicago Bar Assn., December 27, 1921, 8 Am. Bar Assn. J. 34.

9. Act of September 14, 1932, 42 Stat. 838-839. That Act provided also that—

"The senior district judge of each United States district court, on or before the first day of August in each year, shall prepare and submit to the senior circuit judge of the judicial circuit in which said district is situated, a report setting forth the condition of business in said district court, including the number and character of cases on the docket, the business in arrears, and cases disposed of, and such other facts pertinent to the business dispatched and pending as said district judge may deem proper, together with recommendations as to the need of additional judicial assistance for the disposal of business for the year ensuing. Said reports shall be laid before the conference [of senior circuit judges] . . . , by said senior circuit judge, . . . together with such recommendations as he may deem proper." *Id.* 838.

The Conference of Senior Circuit Judges now includes also the Chief Justice of the United States Court of Appeals for the District of Columbia. 50 Stat. 473.

10. 42 Stat. 839. The Act of August 27, 1937, 50 Stat. 753, has strengthened the authorization.

11. Address to American Bar Association at San Francisco, August 10, 1922, 6 J. Am. Jud. Soc. 37; 57 Am. L. Rev. 3, and see 8 Am. Bar Assn. J. 601-602, 47 Am. Bar Assn. Rep. 252.

12. 42 Stat. 837.

13. At the 1946 Conference, the Chief Justice of the United States presided. The ten circuits, plus the District of Columbia, were represented. Five other federal judges reported on special committee assignments. Addresses were made by the Chairman of the Judiciary Committee of the House of Representatives and by the Attorney General. The latter dealt with the Administrative Procedure Act, the Federal Tort Claims Act, the new Federal Rules of Criminal Procedure, the Federal Jury Bills, Youth Offenders' Bill, Public Defenders' Bill, Habeas Corpus Procedural and Jurisdictional Bills and Bills as to reviews of orders of certain administrative agencies. He requested appointment of a committee to consider procedure in cases of juvenile delinquency.

The Seventh Annual Report of the Director of the Administrative Office of the United States Courts was received. It included a Report of the Division of Procedural Studies and Statistics and is printed with the Report of the Conference.

The state of the Dockets of Circuit Courts of Appeals, District Courts and Special Courts was reviewed.

Other matters reviewed, and generally made the subjects of specific recommendations, were those of: Additional Judges; Court Reporters (including changes in basic salaries, description of positions and operating arrangements, and recommendations as to provisions on court reporters in proposed revision of the Judicial Code); Budget Estimates; Bankruptcy Administration, including recommendations as to proposed amendments to the Bankruptcy Act and as to action to be taken at a special meeting of the Conference to be called to deal with the new Referees' Salary Act (this special meeting was held April 21-22, 1947, and final action was taken in time to go into effect July 1, 1947); Review of Orders of Interstate Commerce Commission, other Administrative Agencies and of Three-Judge Courts; Treatment of Insane Persons Charged with Crime in the Federal Courts; Sentencing and Parole of Federal Offenders; Removal of Civil Disabilities of Probationers Under Certain Conditions; Trial of

Minor Offenders by Commissioners; Transfer of Jurisdiction for Supervision of Probationers from Court of Original Jurisdiction to the District of Supervision; Use of Trial Memoranda in Criminal Cases; Habeas Corpus Procedure; Jury System; Representation of Indigent Litigants; Judicial Statistics; Assignments of Judges Outside of their Circuits; Amendments to Admiralty Rules; Disposition of Old Records; Postwar Building Plans for Quarters of the U. S. Courts; Salaries in the Administrative Office of the U. S. Courts; Procedure in Circuit Conferences as to Legislation Affecting District Courts and District Judges; and Keeping of Certain Court Offices Open on Saturday Forenoons. A Conference Committee on Probation with Special Reference to Juvenile Delinquency was added to the existing committees. Two Conference Committees were discharged and all others continued.

14. Mr. Justice Van Devanter estimated that the Court then was "hearing cases on the regular call that have been on the docket about twelve or thirteen months." Hearing before a Subcommittee of the Committee on the Judiciary of the Senate on S. 2060 and 2061, 68th Cong., 1st Sess. 42 (1924). Chief Justice Taft, two years before, had estimated it at eighteen to twenty-four months. See note 1, *supra*.

15. These approximations are based upon the tables as to the Docket of the Supreme Court in Frankfurter and Landis, The Supreme Court Under the Judiciary Act of 1925, 42 Harv. L. Rev. 1, 10, 13.

16. Act of March 3, 1891, §2, 26 Stat. 826.

17. Act of March 3, 1911, §289, 36 Stat. 1167.

18. Act of March 3, 1891, §6, 26 Stat. 828.

19. This Committee consisted of Justices Day and McReynolds, with Chief Justice White as a member *ex officio*. Chief Justice Taft added Mr. Justice Van Devanter to the Committee, and himself pressed the matter vigorously. Upon the retirement of Mr. Justice Day, Mr. Justice Van Devanter became the Committee Chairman and the principal draftsman of the bill. (Chief Justice Taft, 35 Yale L. J. 2.) Mr. Justice Sutherland, a former member of the Senate Committee on the Judiciary, was added to the Committee and the bill was thoroughly explained in Committee Hearings. *E.g.*, Chief Justice Taft, in Hearing before Committee on the Judiciary, House of Representatives, on H. R. 10479, 67th Cong., 2d Sess. 1 (1922); Justices Van Devanter, McReynolds and Sutherland, in Hearing before Subcommittee of Committee on the Judiciary of the Senate, on S. 2060 and 2061, 68th Cong., 1st Sess. 25-62 (1924). Justices Van Devanter, McReynolds and Sutherland, with Chief Justice Taft, in Hearing before Committee on the Judiciary, House of Representatives, on H. R. 8206, 68th Cong., 2d Sess. 6-30 (1924).

For a summary of the nature and effect of this bill and of the service rendered by this Committee, see statement by Charles E. Hughes, Jr., in Proceedings in Memory of Mr. Justice Van Devanter, March 16, 1942, 316 U. S. V, XII-XIV.

20. 43 Stat. 936.

21. Revised Rules of the Supreme Court of the United States, Rule 38

(5), 306 U. S. 718-719. See also, Rule 12 as to Jurisdictional Statements Required in Appeal Cases, 306 U. S. 694, amended 316 U. S. 715.

22. "At the 1937 term 701 petitions [for certiorari] were denied on the merits; at the 1938 term, 666. The 155 petitions granted at the 1937 term were 17.7 percent of the total filed; the 130 at the 1938 term, 16 percent. Like percentages have maintained themselves with singular consistency since prior to the enlargement of discretionary jurisdiction under the Act of 1925. The percentage of petitions granted during the sixteen terms since that of 1923 is 18.1 percent; the term-by-term figures disclose no sustained trend either upward or downward." Hart, The Business of the Supreme Court at the October Terms, 1937 and 1938. 53 Harv. L. Rev. 579, 585. In the foregoing quotation "denied on the merits" means denied on the merits of the petition for certiorari, as distinguished, for example, from a denial because of untimeliness. It does not mean denied on the merits of the case.

The Docket of the Supreme Court for its October 1946 Term shows: petitions for certiorari acted upon (exclusive of those filed *In Forma Pauperis*) 733; of which 148, or about 20.2 percent were granted. The 529 additional cases, treated as petitions for certiorari, but filed *In Forma Pauperis* included the many requests for review received from penitentiary inmates. Only eight, of these 529 "petitions," were found to justify the granting of them. To include these "petitions" would produce a misleading total of 1,262 petitions for certiorari acted upon of which 156, or only 12.4 percent were granted. To avoid this confusion, a change in practice is being put into effect whereby these informal requests will be placed on the Miscellaneous Docket and will be transferred to the General Docket only when and if granted.

"The jurisdiction [of the Supreme Court to review cases by granting a writ of certiorari] was not conferred upon this Court merely to give the defeated party in the Circuit Court of Appeals another hearing. Our experience shows that 80 percent of those who petition for certiorari do not appreciate these necessary limitations upon our issue of the writ." Taft, C. J., in *Magnum Co.* v. *Coty*, 262 U. S. 159, 163.

"I think that it is safe to say that about 60 percent of the applications for certiorari are wholly without merit and ought never to have been made. There are probably about 20 percent or so in addition which have a fair degree of plausibility, but which fail to survive a critical examination. The remainder, falling short, I believe, of 20 percent, show substantial grounds and are granted. I think that [it] is the view of the members of the Court that if any error is made in dealing with these applications it is on the side of liberality." Hughes, C. J., in a letter to Senator Burton K. Wheeler, March 23, 1937, reprinted in 81 Cong. Rec. 2814-2815 (1937).

23. "For instance, if there were five votes against granting the petition and four in favor of granting it, it would be granted, because we proceed upon the theory that when as many as four members of the court, and even three in some instances, are impressed with the propriety of our taking the case the petition should be granted. This is the uniform way in which petitions for writs of certiorari are considered." Mr. Justice Van Devanter testifying before a Subcommittee of the Committee on the Judiciary of the Senate on S. 2060 and 2061, 68th Cong., 1st Sess. 29 (1924).

See also, statements by Justices Van Devanter and Brandeis on Hearings before Senate Committee on the Judiciary on S. 2176, 74th Cong., 1st Sess. 9-10 (1935).

"In all matters before the Court, except in the mere routine of administration, all the Justices—unless for some reason a Justice is disqualified or unable to act in a particular case—participate in the decision. This applies to the grant or refusal of petitions for certiorari, which are granted if four Justices think they should be. A vote by a majority is not required in such cases. Even if two or three of the Justices are strongly of the opinion that certiorari should be allowed, frequently the other Justices will acquiesce in their view, but the petition is always granted if four so vote." Hughes, C. J., in a letter to Senator Burton K. Wheeler, March 23, 1937, reprinted in 81 Cong. Rec. 2814 (1937).

"But as we have adhered to our long standing practice of granting certiorari upon the affirmative vote of four Justices, the case is properly here for decision and is, I think, correctly decided." Stone, C. J., in *Bailey* v. *Central Vermont R. Co.*, 319 U. S. 350, 359.

That three votes were not sufficient to grant, see *Scarborough* v. *Pennsylvania R. Co.*, 326 U. S. 755; *Helvering* v. *Sprouse*, 315 U. S. 810; and *Simmons* v. *Peavy-Welsh Lumber Co.*, 311 U. S. 685. And see Boskey, Mechanics of the Supreme Court's Certiorari Jurisdiction, 46 Col. L. Rev. 255, 257.

24. "All cases submitted, and all business before the Court, at this term, having been disposed of,

"It is now here ordered by this Court that all cases on the docket be, and they are hereby, continued to the next term." (1929) Sup. Ct. J. 311.

"At the last term the Court disposed of every case that was ripe for decision. For the first time in many years no case that had been submitted was allowed to go over." Frankfurter and Landis, The Business of the Supreme Court at October Term, 1929, 44 Harv. L. Rev. 1, 2.

"The Supreme Court is fully abreast of its work. . . .

". . . We shall be able to hear all these cases [twenty-eight awaiting argument March 23, 1937], and such others as may come up for argument, before our adjournment for the term. There is no congestion of cases upon our calendar.

"This gratifying condition has obtained for several years. We have been able for several terms to adjourn after disposing of all cases which are ready to be heard." Hughes, C. J., in a letter to Senator Burton K. Wheeler, March 23, 1937, reprinted in 81 Cong. Rec. 2814 (1937). This letter also tabulates the case load for O. T. 1930-O. T. 1935.

25. Frankfurter and Landis, The Business of the Supreme Court at October Term, 1930, 45 Harv. L. Rev. 271, 274.

26. Frankfurter and Hart, The Business of the Supreme Court at October Term, 1932, 47 Harv. L. Rev. 245, 249.

In the proceedings held in the Supreme Court in memory of Chief Justice Taft, on June 1, 1931, Chief Justice Hughes said:

"Deeply concerned with improvements in administration, the Chief Justice gave special attention to his own duty as administrator. Even the distinction of his contribution to the jurisprudence of the Court does not obscure, but throws into a stronger light, by reason of his versatility, his preeminence in the executive department of its work. In the successful endeavor to end the delays which bring such a deserved reproach upon judicial procedure, he was ever a leader, and he would have been the first to recognize the able support which he received from his colleagues in this effort. It was not a vain attempt to bring the Court up to its work by a spasmodic activity, but the intelligent formulation of a plan which, receiving the sanction of Congress, has put the Court, we trust permanently, upon a basis by which it can keep abreast of the demands upon it. So long as we follow the example which he has set and avail ourselves of the opportunity which his leadership provided, the delays of justice will have no countenance or illustration here.

"But the Chief Justice was not content with expediting the work of this Court. He felt a special responsibility with respect to the entire Federal judicial system. Many years before he came to this bench, he had suggested that either the Supreme Court or the Chief Justice should have an adequate executive force to keep current watch upon the business awaiting dispatch in all the districts and circuits of the United States and to make a periodical estimate of the number of judges needed in the various districts and to make the requisite assignments. In a different manner, it was sought to attain the object he had in view by the establishment, in 1922, through his persistence, of the Judicial Conference of the Senior Circuit Judges, held annually, at which the Chief Justice of this Court presides, and which considers the needs of judicial service in the different districts and makes recommendations accordingly. This is an instrumentality of great value, and what it has accomplished and the promise of what it may achieve are due in the largest measure to the foresight and intelligent guidance of Chief Justice Taft." 285 U. S. XXXIV-XXXV.

27. I Warren, The Supreme Court in United States History (1935) 169-171; II Warren (1937) 362.

28. Acquisition of site authorized, Act of May 25, 1926, 44 Stat. 630; appropriation of $1,500,000 approved, Act of February 28, 1927, 44 Stat. 1254; increased by $268,741, Act of March 4, 1929, 45 Stat. 1614. The acquisition of land was completed November 25, 1929, the largest parcel being that purchased from the National Woman's Party, often referred to as the Little Brick Capitol, which had been used for meetings of Congress after the British had burned the Capitol in 1814. Final Report of the United States Supreme Court Building Commission, Sen. Doc. No. 88, 76th Cong., 1st Sess. 1-2 (1939).

29. The United States Supreme Court Building Commission originally consisted of: Chairman: Hon. William Howard Taft, Chief Justice of the United States. Members: Hon. Willis Van Devanter, Associate Justice of the Supreme Court of the United States; Hon. Henry W. Keyes, Chairman of the Senate Committee on Public Buildings and Grounds; Hon. James A. Reed, ranking minority member of the Senate Committee on Public Buildings and Grounds; Hon. Richard N. Elliott, Chairman of the House Committee on Public Buildings and Grounds; Hon. Fritz G. Lanham, ranking minority member of the House Committee on Public Buildings and Grounds; Hon. David Lynn, Architect of the Capitol.

At the conclusion of its service, it consisted of: Chairman: Hon. Charles Evans Hughes, Chief Justice of the United States. Members: Hon. Willis Van Devanter, Associate Justice (retired); Hon. Tom Connally, Senator from Texas; Hon. James A. Reed, former Senator from Missouri; Hon. Richard N. Elliott, former Representative from Indiana; Hon. Fritz G. Lanham, Representative from Texas. Member and executive officer: Hon. David Lynn, Architect of the Capitol. Final Report of the United States Supreme Court Building Commission, Sen. Doc. No. 88, 76th Cong., 1st Sess. 4 (1939).

30. Appropriation for building and grounds, including furniture, furnishings and equipment $9,740,000.00
Expended for building, treatment of grounds, furniture, furnishings and equipment 9,646,467.98
Unexpended and unobligated balance June 6, 1939 ... $93,532.02

Final Report of the United States Supreme Court Building Commission, Sen. Doc. No. 88, 76th Cong., 1st Sess. 21 (1939).

31. Address at Cincinnati Law School Commencement, May 23, 1941, 5 Ky. L. J. 1, 14. See also, his recommendation of uniform federal rules of practice, both in law and equity, made as Chief Justice, in the Hearings before the Senate Committee on the Judiciary on S. 2432, 2433 and 2523, 67th Cong., 1st Sess. 16-17 (1921).

32. Act of June 19, 1934, 48 Stat. 1064, 28 U. S. C. §§723b, 723c.

33. The Advisory Committee appointed by the Supreme Court to assist it in drafting a unified system of Equity and Law Rules and to serve without compensation consisted of: William D. Mitchell, of New York City, Chairman; Scott M. Loftin, of Jacksonville, Florida, President of the American Bar Association; George W. Wickersham, of New York City, President of the American Law Institute; Wilbur H. Cherry, of Minneapolis, Minnesota, Professor of Law at the University of Minnesota; Charles E. Clark, of New Haven, Connecticut, Dean of the Law School of Yale University; Armistead M. Dobie, of University, Virginia, Dean of the Law School of the University of Virginia; Robert G. Dodge, of Boston, Massachusetts; George Donworth, of Seattle, Washington; Joseph G. Gamble, of Des Moines, Iowa; Monte M. Lemann, of New Orleans, Louisiana; Edmund M. Morgan, of Cambridge, Massachusetts, Professor of Law at Harvard University; Warren Olney, Jr., of San Francisco, California; Edson R. Sunderland, of Ann Arbor, Michigan, Professor of Law at the University of Michigan; and Edgar B. Tolman, of Chicago, Illinois. Charles E. Clark was appointed Reporter to the Advisory Committee. 295 U. S. 774-775.

34. Notes were published with the Committee's Preliminary Draft of May, 1936. They were revised and published with the Committee's Report of April, 1937, and revised again to conform to the Committee's Final Report of November, 1937, and to the Rules as approved by the Supreme Court, December 20, 1937. Federal Rules of Civil Procedure 215. These Rules were reported to Congress by the Attorney General, January 3, 1938, and took effect on September 16, 1938, three months after adjourn-

ment of the second regular session of the 75th Congress on June 16, 1938. See Rule 86 and 52 Stat. 1454. 308 U. S. 645-788, 28 U. S. C. fol. §723c.

Rule 81 (a) (6) was amended December 28, 1939, 308 U. S. 642, 28 U. S. C. fol. §723c. See also, amendments adopted by the Supreme Court December 27, 1946, and reported to Congress by the Attorney General January 3, 1947, 16 S. Ct. Digest (1947 Cum. 5).

35. The Supreme Court was authorized by the Act of June 29, 1940, 54 Stat. 688, 18 U. S. C. §687, to prescribe new Federal Rules of Criminal Procedure for the District Courts of the United States. On February 3, 1941, the Court appointed the following Advisory Committee on Rules in Criminal Cases to serve without compensation: Arthur T. Vanderbilt, Newark, New Jersey, Chairman; James J. Robinson, Professor of Law at the Indiana University Law School, Reporter; Alexander Holtzoff, Washington, D. C., Secretary; Newman F. Baker, Professor of Law at the Northwestern University Law School; George James Burke, Ann Arbor, Michigan; John J. Burns, Boston, Massachusetts; Frederick E. Crane, New York City; Gordon Dean, Washington, D. C.; George H. Dession, Professor of Law at the Yale Law School; Sheldon Glueck, Professor of Law at the Harvard Law School; George Z. Medalie, New York City; Lester B. Orfield, Professor of Law at the University of Nebraska Law School; Murray Seasongood, Cincinnati, Ohio; J. O. Seth, Santa Fe, New Mexico; John B. Waite, Professor of Law at the University of Michigan Law School; Herbert Wechsler, Professor of Law at the Columbia Law School; and G. Aaron Youngquist, Minneapolis, Minnesota. 312 U. S. 717-718.

After the consideration of several drafts, the Supreme Court, on December 26, 1944, prescribed the new Rules. 323 U. S. 821. These were filed with Congress January 3, 1945, and took effect March 21, 1946, three months after the adjournment of the first regular session of the 79th Congress on December 21, 1945. See Rule 59 and 59 Stat. 849. 327 U. S. 821, 18 U. S. C. A. fol. §687, 1946 Pocket Part 205.

36. Chapter XV, entitled "The Administration of the United States Courts," was added to the Judicial Code by the Act of August 7, 1939, effective November 6, 1939. 53 Stat. 1223, 28 U. S. C. §§444-450.

37. 308 U. S. 642, 641.

II

The Cornerstone of Constitutional Law

THE EXTRAORDINARY CASE OF *MARBURY* v. *MADISON**

ONE HUNDRED AND FIFTY YEARS AGO, the feud between
the Federalists, led by President Adams, and the Anti-
Federalists, led by Vice President Jefferson, was at fever
heat. Until the adjournment of Congress in May, General
John Marshall of Virginia had been serving his first and only
term as a Federalist member of the House of Representatives.
In June, he became Secretary of State and supported President Adams throughout his bitter and unsuccessful campaign
for reelection.

The Anti-Federalists carried enough states to elect Jefferson in the electoral college. However, that cumbersome
institution was still operating under the original provision
whereby each elector must vote for two candidates for President. The candidate receiving the highest vote was to become President and the next highest Vice President. The
Anti-Federalists had expected to elect Jefferson President
and Aaron Burr Vice President. Nevertheless, their electors
all voted for both, with the result that Jefferson received
seventy-three votes, Burr seventy-three, Adams sixty-five,
Pinckney sixty-four and Jay one. This threw the election into the House of Representatives where a majority of the
sixteen states, each casting one vote, was necessary for a
choice. Finally, on February 17, 1801, two weeks before his
inauguration, Jefferson was chosen President on the thirty-
sixth ballot. This was after Federalist Hamilton, who disapproved of both candidates, threw his influence to Jefferson as the less dangerous of the two. Marshall declined to
express a preference.

* Reprinted by permission of the American Bar Association Journal.

Adams Appoints Marshall to Supreme Bench

In the meantime the Federalists had concentrated their hopes for the survival of the Republic upon the federal judiciary. The Supreme Court consisted of six Federalists. Four had been appointed by Washington. They were Chief Justice Ellsworth of Connecticut and Associate Justices Cushing of Massachusetts, Paterson of New Jersey and Chase of Maryland. Two had been appointed by Adams. They were Bushrod Washington of Virginia and Moore of North Carolina. Chief Justice Ellsworth was in France, doubling as Minister to France. Being in ill health, he resigned as Chief Justice in time to give President Adams a chance to appoint a Federalist successor. The President promptly named former Chief Justice Jay to the vacancy. With equal promptness, Jay declined the appointment. On January 20, the President made a surprise appointment of his Secretary of State, John Marshall, to the Chief Justiceship. He was confirmed January 27 and, on February 4, 1801, entered upon his duties. He continued to serve also, without salary however, as Secretary of State to the end of President Adams' term on March 3, 1801. He was succeeded by James Madison on March 5. Almost the first official duty performed by John Marshall, as Chief Justice, was his administration of the oath of office to Thomas Jefferson, on March 4, 1801.

"Midnight Judges" Appointed as One of Adams' Last Presidential Acts

In the midst of this embroilment the Federalists in Congress, on February 13, 1801, had passed a new Circuit Court Bill. On its merits this seems to have been a well-considered bill intended to do away with the need for circuit duty by the Justices of the Supreme Court and to provide circuit judges to assume those duties. This would speed up the delayed litigation in the circuits. It also would do away with the embarrassment of the constant presence on the Supreme Court of Justices who had heard the same cases on circuit. To accomplish this, it authorized the appointment of sixteen additional federal judges and President Adams at once filled all those vacancies with Federalists. The nominees were confirmed by the Senate on March 2. Their commissions were signed by President Adams and sealed by his Secretary of State, John Marshall, on March 3. These were nicknamed the "midnight judges." Occasionally it is erroneously thought that their commissions were the ones that became the subject of the *Marbury* v. *Madison* litigation.

The fact is that the case of *Marbury* v. *Madison* arose out of a distinct but somewhat comparable situation. It arose from the passage, on February 27, 1801, of the District of Columbia Organic Act and appointments under it. That act provided for the appointment by the President of justices of the peace, for five-year terms, for the respective counties of Washington and Alexandria within the District. The President did not overlook this opportunity. On March 2, he nominated forty-two such justices of the peace—twenty-three for Washington and nineteen for Alexandria. They were confirmed by the Senate and their commissions were signed by the President and sealed by Secretary Marshall before midnight, March 3. They were the "midnight justices of the peace." Some of these commissions were delivered to the appointees on the night of March 3 by Marshall's brother, James, but not all were delivered. Among those not delivered was that of William Marbury of the County of Washington. It was his claim to that commission, together with the claims of three other similarly situated appointees, that became the subjects of the famous litigation.

In the midst of these extraordinary circumstances, the Supreme Court, on February 2, 1801, met for its first time in Washington. It met in the single section of the Capitol which had been built. That section consisted of a square building immediately north of the future dome. It now stands between the dome and the Senate wing. The Senate met in the East front room, the House met at the rear. The Court occupied a committee room 24 feet wide and 30 feet long. That room later became the office of the Marshal of the Court. There Chief Justice Marshall, on February 4, 1801, at the age of forty-four, assumed his duties. The Court passed on several motions, handed down no reported opinions and adjourned on February 10. At its next Term in August, 1801, the Court handed down one opinion. Instead of the several Justices rendering separate opinions, *seriatim*, as had been the custom, the new Chief Justice spoke for the Court as a unit. Thereafter, until 1805, each opinion was delivered in that manner, except in two instances where the Chief Justice had participated in the case on the circuit.

Marbury Case Expected to Lead to Impeachment of Judges

The Court met again in December, 1801. It was then that the Marbury litigation was started. The attorney for Marbury was Charles Lee. Until recently Lee had been Attorney General under President Adams. The Marbury proceeding was instituted by a motion for a rule to show cause why a writ of mandamus should not issue to direct James Madison, as Secretary of State, to deliver to Marbury a commission as a justice of the peace. The Court ordered Madison to show such cause on the fourth day of the next Term. It was expected that the next Term would be held in June under the new Circuit Court Act. This expectation was not fulfilled, because Congress, with the obvious purpose of preventing the Court from passing so soon on this and other highly controversial issues, abolished the June Term and prescribed Annual Terms meeting in February. Accordingly, Marbury's case was heard in February, 1803, after an extraordinary interval of about fourteen months between succeeding Terms of Court.[1]

The Jefferson Administration regarded the Marbury suit as a brazen attempt to induce the Supreme Court to interfere unlawfully with the conduct of the Executive Branch of the Government. While the Administration believed the judiciary to be without constitutional right to issue a mandamus against the Secretary of State, nevertheless it feared that the Federalist Justices on the Supreme Court would attempt to assert that right. If the Justices did so, some Anti-Federalists indicated that those Justices would render themselves subject to impeachment.

At the same time that this situation existed as to the midnight justices of the peace, an even more serious situation arose as to the sixteen new circuit judges. The Anti-Federalists, outraged by the appointment of these Federalist judges, determined to repeal the entire new Circuit Court Act. While not removing the new judges from their offices, Congress would thus abolish the offices and eliminate the judgeships. Their plan was to restore, in large measure, the terms of the Judiciary Act of 1789. The plan also would return the Justices of the Supreme Court to their circuit duties.

On January 6, 1802, Senator Breckenridge of Kentucky accordingly sought the repeal of the Circuit Court Act which had been passed less than a year before. The repeal bill was fully and ably debated in both Houses. It passed the Senate sixteen to fifteen and the House fifty-nine to thirty-two, becoming law March 31, 1802. The midnight judges protested to Congress but did not litigate their claims. The arguments on the bill, however, had dealt with those claims at length. Those discussions explored fully the constitutional right of Congress to abolish courts to which judges already had been appointed.

The debate also had reviewed the fundamental issue of the

right to a judicial review of the constitutional validity of any Act of Congress. The latter issue was the great issue to which the Court subsequently addressed itself in deciding *Marbury* v. *Madison*. The Anti-Federalists insisted that Congress was the equal of the courts and that the Constitution gave no power of judicial review over the constitutional validity of Acts of Congress. The Federalists insisted, with equal vigor, that such a power was vested in the courts by the Constitution. The Anti-Federalists confidently expected that the six Federalist members of the Supreme Court would take the latter view. They expected also that the Court would attempt to apply that power of review to the repealer that Congress had passed and would find some ground upon which to declare that repealer to be constitutionally invalid. The Anti-Federalists expected also that the Court would challenge the power of the Executive to withhold a commission from Marbury. Furthermore, it was suggested that, if the Court asserted such power over the Legislative and Executive Branches of the Government, this assertion would provide Congress with the necessary basis for the impeachment of the offending Justices and for their removal from office. The extraordinary thing is that Chief Justice Marshall found a way to announce and establish the principle of judicial review in both of these fields without making an immediate application of it hostile to the Administration and without providing the expected basis for impeachment proceedings.

Although the circuit judges declined to press, on their own account, the issue of the constitutionality of the repeal of the Circuit Court Act, the Supreme Court could not avoid the issue. Even before the Court assembled for its new February Term in 1803, the Justices were obliged to decide whether to resume their duties on circuit or to refuse to do so. By a majority conclusion, ascertained by correspondence, the Justices determined to resume, without controversy, the circuit duties which had been terminated by the Act of 1801 but had been reimposed by the Act of 1802.[2]

Unusual Features of the Trial of Marbury v. Madison

Such was the extraordinary background for the trial of *Marbury* v. *Madison* in February, 1803. There were further unusual features connected with the trial itself. The first such feature, judged by the practice today, was the unhesitating and apparently unquestioned participation of Chief Justice Marshall in the trial. Assuming that the Court had jurisdiction of the case and had a right to issue a writ of mandamus to the Secretary of State, the issue between the parties turned upon the right of Marbury to secure possession of the very commission which the Chief Justice, as Secretary of State, had sealed on March 3, 1801, but which the Chief Justice's brother had not delivered when he delivered others on that night. It also appears from John Marshall's correspondence with his brother that, as Secretary of State, John Marshall believed that these appointments were complete with the affixation to them of the Seal of the United States and that the subsequent recordings and deliveries of the commissions were not essential to the appointments. As Chief Justice, he later stated that conclusion in the opinion of the Court.

Furthermore, while the report of this case at 1 Cranch 137 shows no absence of Justices from the Court at this trial, the minutes of the Court do not record Justice Cushing as present at any trial session or on the date of handing down the decision. Apparently, he did not participate in the case. The minutes also show that Justice Moore was present on February 24 when the decision was announced but they do not record his presence on February 10 or 11 when they show that the case was before the Court for hearing and argument.[3] Accordingly, on those two days, if the Chief Justice had disqualified himself, there would not have been the required quorum of four present.

Jefferson's Attorney General, Levi Lincoln, participated only as a witness. He answered some but not all the questions submitted to him. Those questions were reduced to writing at his request and the Court allowed him until the next day to determine what response, if any, he should make to them. The Court heard at least three other witnesses and read a material affidavit from James Marshall, the brother of the Chief Justice. All this testimony related to the signing, sealing and failure to deliver the commissions. The Court then heard an argument by Mr. Lee for the petitioners, both on the question of jurisdiction and on the merits. No argument was made in opposition and no one officially represented the Secretary of State in the proceeding.

Finally, and quite in keeping with the extraordinary circumstances surrounding this leading case in American constitutional law, it now appears that, although this proceeding was entered on the Court docket and notations were made showing that certain hearings were held, the Court today has no file on the case and no papers relating to it. The rule to show cause was marked "discharged the Court not having jurisdiction to issue a Mandamus in this case." If it were not for the careful reporting of the case by William Cranch and the informal newspaper reports of the opinion rendered, we, today, would have no reliable record of the fundamental legal principles then announced by the Court and which have become of primary significance in American constitutional law.[4]

Marshall's Opinion Itself Was Extraordinary

Even more extraordinary than the background and the trial of *Marbury* v. *Madison* is the opinion that was rendered. This was read February 24, 1803, by the Chief Justice on behalf of the Court. It made no reference to the absence of

Justice Cushing throughout the case or to the absence of Justice Moore during the hearings. It was the first major opinion announced for the Court by Chief Justice Marshall, although he had announced one extended opinion at the August Term, 1801, and four opinions at the December Term, 1801.

Charles Warren, in his invaluable work *The Supreme Court in United States History*, says of this opinion:

> To the lawyers of today, the significance of Marshall's opinion lies in its establishment of the power of the Court to adjudicate the validity of an Act of Congress—the fundamental decision in the American system of constitutional law. To the public of 1803, on the other hand, the case represented the determination of Marshall and his Associates to interfere with the authority of the Executive, and it derived its chief importance then from that aspect."[5]

Senator Beveridge, in his colorful work entitled *The Life of John Marshall*, says of this case:

> A case was then pending [1802] before the Supreme Court the decision of which might, by boldness and ingenuity, be made to serve as the occasion for that tribunal's assertion of its right and power to invalidate acts of Congress and also for the laying-down of rules for the guidance of all departments of the Government. This was the case of *Marbury* v. *Madison*.[6]

Chief Justice's Opinion Was Bold and Ingenious

The Chief Justice amply supplied the required boldness and ingenuity. In his discussion of the case in the opinion of the Court, he reversed the usual order of consideration of the issues. Instead of taking up the jurisdictional question first, the Court discussed the merits first. After finding that there would be merit to the petition if it were addressed to a proper court, the Supreme Court then discussed its own jurisdiction of the case. On finding a lack of jurisdiction in itself, the Court discharged the rule to show cause but handed down in its opinion a chart on the merits of the case for the guidance of any lower court to which this or a similar case might be presented.

The opinion presented and answered three questions:

1. *Did the applicant have a right to the commission he demanded? To this the Court answered yes.* It stated that the commission was mere evidence of an appointment. It added that an appointment by the President to an office, not terminable at the will of the President, was certainly complete upon confirmation by the Senate, plus also the President's signature of the commission and the Secretary of State's affixation of the Seal of the United States. The delivery of the commission was not a part of the appointment. The possession of the commission was not essential to the performance of the duties of the office. The appointment was not contingent upon its acceptance. To withhold the commission from the appointee violated his vested legal right to it.

2. *If the applicant had a right to the commission and that right were violated, did the laws of his country afford him a remedy? The Court again answered yes.* It said:

> The government of the United States has been emphatically termed a government of laws, and not of men. It will certainly cease to deserve this high appellation, if the laws furnish no remedy for the violation of a vested legal right.[7]

The Court found nothing to justify putting the head of a department above the laws of his country under circumstances where his duties were prescribed by those laws. The Court sharply distinguished this case from cases concerning political or discretionary acts of the President. It distinguished this case also from those concerning acts done by a Secretary of State for a President as the President's agent, or concerning acts of a Secretary of State that were political or

confidential in their nature. It said that no court would interfere with such acts. However, where specific duties were
assigned by law and individual rights depended upon their
performance, it said that the person injured by the nonper-
formance of those required acts had a right to resort to the
laws of his country to secure their performance. The Court
identified this case as one of that nature.

3. *If those laws thus afforded the applicant a remedy, was
it by way of a writ of mandamus issuing from this Court?
The Court separated this question into two parts. The first
related to the nature of the writ. The second related to the
power of the Court. It then found that mandamus was the
proper writ for this purpose and that it made no difference
that the offender was the Secretary of State.* The Court said:
"It is not by the office of the person to whom the writ is
directed, but the nature of the thing to be done that the
propriety or impropriety of issuing a mandamus, is to be
determined."[8]

*The final question asked was whether the writ could issue
from the Supreme Court as an original writ in this case. To
the surprise of the Administration, the Court answered this
question in the negative.* Having thus held itself to be without jurisdiction, the Supreme Court discharged its rule to
show cause why the writ should not issue. The Court thus
created no immediate conflict between the Executive and
Judicial Branches of the Government. It thus decided the
case in favor of Madison and this made it difficult for the
Administration to object strenuously to the result.

At the same time, as a consequence of its discharge of the
rule for lack of jurisdiction, the statements of the Court on
the merits of the case became unnecessary to the decision.
Those statements could, therefore, be regarded as *obiter
dictum*, although dealing with an issue which had been
argued to the Court by the petitioner and would have been
material if jurisdiction had been established. The interesting

fact is that this statement, unnecessary as it was to the decision, was promptly and widely accepted as the controlling law in such a case. Unorthodox as the procedure was, its justification can be judged only in the light of the times. It is impossible, after 150 years, to evaluate accurately the considerations of public policy that led to the adoption of this course. Judging pragmatically from its ultimate results, the course stands justified. It repulsed successfully, at a critical moment, a serious attack on the Court and the Constitution. The Court disarmed its opponents by deciding the case unexpectedly in their favor. The Court, however, so well expounded its own views on the merits of the case that it successfully clarified the issue and defined a workable relationship between coordinate branches of the Government. The Court displayed such a fairness between the parties that it strengthened public confidence in itself. Evidently, the Court supplied precisely what the conditions required. The need was for a convincing lecture on constitutional law upholding the essential power of the Court, while saving the face of the Chief Executive. The litigation was not pressed further. In fact, one of President Jefferson's later criticisms was that the case actually was moot. By the time the petition had been reached for decision, Marbury's five-year term had nearly half expired. The emoluments of the office were small and the public need for justices of the peace had been largely met by President Jefferson's appointments of new justices of the peace, including many of the original forty-two.

Ultimate Importance of the Case Was Not Seen in 1803

This part of the case which, in 1803, loomed the largest is not the great cornerstone of American constitutional law that the Court's opinion is said to have set in place forever.

The ultimate and major significance of the case is found in the reasons which the Court gave for holding that it had no jurisdiction. It held that it had no jurisdiction to issue the writ because, although Congress had attempted to give the Court power to do so, the Constitution forbade the grant of such a power to this Court in this kind of a case. The Court rested this conclusion on two considerations. The first was that Congress had attempted, by statute, to give the Supreme Court this power. The second, and historically more important consideration, was that the attempt was void because the Court determined that the statute violated the Constitution. This ruling was based squarely upon the Court's right of final judicial review of the constitutional validity of congressional action.

The Court felt the need for an immediate authoritative clarification of the constitutional relationship on this point between the Judicial and the Legislative Branches of the Government. If these branches of the Government were each to be an independent but final judge of the constitutional validity of Acts of Congress, chaos was around the corner. It was necessary for a single umpire to be recognized to decide whether or not the Acts of Congress were made in pursuance to the Constitution. The President and perhaps a majority of Congress were opposed to such a right of judicial review. It was intimated that they might regard a decision by the Court against them on that issue as such a usurpation of power by the judiciary that it would justify the impeachment and removal of the Justices making it. It was under these conditions that the Supreme Court announced its opinion in *Marbury* v. *Madison*, unequivocally, emphatically and repeatedly supporting its right of judicial review. The opinion was convincingly phrased. Furthermore, it was applied in this particular case so as to produce an order favorable to, rather than hostile to, President Jefferson and to Secretary Madison. The Administration thus won the case, solely because the Court found unconstitutional the very Act of Congress upon which depended the Court's authority to issue the writ.

[35]

MILLS COLLEGE
LIBRARY

The great objective of the Court was to secure widespread recognition of the principle of the judicial review of the constitutionality of Acts of Congress. Chief Justice Marshall stated the position of the Court with persuasiveness. Having described the Constitution as the expression of the original right of the people to establish their own government, he said for the Court:

> The constitution is either a superior, paramount law, unchangeable by ordinary means, or it is on a level with ordinary legislative acts, and like other acts, is alterable when the legislature shall please to alter it.
>
> If the former part of the alternative be true, then a legislative act contrary to the constitution is not law: if the latter part be true, then written constitutions are absurd attempts, on the part of the people, to limit a power, in its own nature illimitable.
>
> Certainly all those who have framed written constitutions contemplate them as forming the fundamental and paramount law of the nation, and consequently the theory of every such government must be, that an act of the legislature, repugnant to the constitution, is void.[9]

The opinion repeated these statements in several ways, then the Court concluded as follows:

> It is also not entirely unworthy of observation, that in declaring what shall be the *supreme* law of the land, the *constitution* itself is first mentioned; and not the laws of the United States generally, but those only which shall be made in *pursuance* of the constitution, have that rank.
>
> Thus, the particular phraseology of the constitution of the United States confirms and strengthens the principle, supposed to be essential to all written constitutions, that a law repugnant to the constitution is void; and that *courts*, as well as other departments, are bound by that instrument.[10]

Upon this rock the nation has been built.

It makes an anticlimax to say more. However, from a lawyer's point of view, it is important to note the reasoning by which the Court brought the doctrine of judicial review into this case. To do this, it was necessary for the Court to establish two points.

Neither of these points had been presented on argument. It must have been a substantial surprise to many when the Court based its decision squarely upon them.

These two points were:

(1) That *Section 13 of the Judiciary Act of 1789 attempted* to give the Supreme Court power to issue a writ of mandamus *in an original proceeding* against an officer of the United States, including the Secretary of State.

(2) That *Article III of the Constitution prohibited* the grant of such a power by Congress to the Supreme Court.

We are not concerned here whether, as a new question, either or both of these conclusions would be supportable. It is enough for our present purposes that the Court expressly upheld them. Without them, the principle of the judicial review of the constitutional validity of a statute would not have been material to this case. With them, that principle became material.

It is an appropriate part, however, of any study of the extraordinary features of this case to note how bold each of these propositions was and how the Court might have found a way to discharge the rule to show cause on statutory grounds without relying on, or raising, the great constitutional issue.

The fact is that Section 13 of the Judiciary Act of 1789, which purported to define the original jurisdiction of the Supreme Court, could have been interpreted as not attempting to extend the jurisdiction of the Supreme Court to the issuance of a writ of mandamus in an original proceeding. It has been suggested that this clause merely extended the remedy of mandamus to the cases over which the Court already had jurisdiction, and that the clause accordingly did not enlarge the Court's jurisdiction.[11] In the face of the subsequently demonstrated constitutional objections to the broad interpretation of this clause which was adopted by the Court, there is much to be said for the narrower interpretation suggested. If the narrower interpretation were adopted, the rule would have been discharged for lack of jurisdiction. The ground for discharge would have been the simple absence of statutory, as well as constitutional, provision for it. There thus would have been no issue in the case as to the constitutionality of any statute and there would have been no opportunity to expound the doctrine of judicial review of that constitutionality.

The success of the Chief Justice in discovering and announcing the Court's broad construction of Section 13, which was in conflict with the Constitution, is all the more extraordinary when the sponsorship of Section 13 is recalled. That section was a part of the Judiciary Act of 1789. Its authorship is attributed to Senator Oliver Ellsworth, who had been a delegate to the Constitutional Convention of 1787, and who was the Chief Justice of the Supreme Court who immediately preceded Marshall. It was a bold step to assert that, in spite of such sponsorship, this section was an attempt by Congress to enlarge the original jurisdiction of the Supreme Court beyond its constitutional limits. Equally striking is the conversion of Justice Paterson to the interpretation of Section 13 adopted by the Chief Justice. Justice Paterson, as a Senator from New Jersey, had been associated with Senator Ellsworth on the Judiciary Committee which had sponsored this Act. He also had been a delegate to the Constitutional Convention of 1787, not to mention the New Jersey Convention that ratified the Federal Constitution. Obviously, neither of these men knowingly would have sought, by statute, to enlarge the Court's jurisdiction beyond the constitutional limit of that jurisdiction.

Finally, assuming that the statute was an attempted enlargement of the Court's original jurisdiction, the Chief Justice's constitutional argument to establish its invalidity was also a bold one. Under the leadership of the Chief Justice, the Court found in the *limited affirmative statement* of the Court's original jurisdiction an *implied negative that all other original jurisdiction was denied* to the Court. The Court admitted that, standing alone, the limited affirmative scope of the Court's jurisdiction covering its original proceedings did not necessarily exclude all other original jurisdiction. The Court stated, however, that it was convinced, by the next clause, that it did so. That clause added the statement that in "*all the other Cases* before mentioned, the Supreme Court shall have *appellate Jurisdiction,* both as to Law and Fact, *with such Exceptions,* and under such Regulations *as the Congress shall make.*" (Italics supplied.) The Court said that this meant that in all those other cases the Court's jurisdiction was to be *solely appellate and not original.* The exceptions which could be made by Congress might omit some of this appellate jurisdiction of the Supreme Court but apparently Congress could not, by way of an exception, convert any of that appellate jurisdiction into original jurisdiction. This point is not mentioned here to discuss its strength or weakness. It is mentioned only to show how resolutely the Court pushed away another possible disposition of the case and faced, with readiness, the issue of the unconstitutionality of the jurisdictional statute.

In the week following that in which the opinion in *Marbury* v. *Madison* was announced, the Court again disarmed its opposition by its decision in *Stuart* v. *Laird.*[12] The Court there applied the doctrine of judicial review to the statute which had repealed the Circuit Court Act of 1801 and had terminated the existence of courts on which the midnight judges had been appointed to serve. The Supreme Court upheld the constitutional validity of that repealer. This decision made it still more difficult for the Anti-Federalists to claim that there was great danger in the doctrine of judicial review.

The battle, however, was resumed later along another front. On February 4, 1805, nearly two years after the decision in *Marbury* v. *Madison*, the House of Representatives impeached Justice Chase of the Supreme Court. The charges related primarily to his conduct on the circuit. The arguments made against him also reflected a view that impeachment was not merely a punitive process but an inquest of office. After extended debate, a majority of the Senate, on March 1, acquitted Justice Chase on five of the eight counts. On the other three, an actual majority, but not the required two-thirds, voted for his conviction. This failure to convict disposed of impeachment as a ready means of legislative recall of federal judges. The right of the Court to be independent in its judgments, as well as its right to review the constitutional validity of the Acts of Congress, was thus sustained.

NOTES TO CHAPTER II

1. The minutes show that a session of the Court was held at the Capitol, "agreeably to the Statute," August 2, 1802. Only Justice Chase was present and the only action taken was to continue twenty-five cases, including *Marbury* v. *Madison*, until the next Term.

2. They questioned the validity of the congressional imposition of these circuit duties upon Supreme Court Justices in the face of the Constitution's implication that the inferior courts be separate from the Supreme Court. They felt bound, however, by the acquiescence of the original Supreme Court in the performance of such duties under the Judiciary Act of 1789. See *Stuart* v. *Laird*, 1 Cranch 299.

3. The minutes show Justice Moore was present February 12, 18, 19, 21, 22, 23 and 24, 1803, and one of the docket books indicates that witnesses appeared February 10 and 12.

4. William Cranch was then an assistant judge of the Circuit Court of the District of Columbia. It is due to his initiative that the report of this case is so well preserved. He states in the preface to his reports that before

this February Term, 1803, he had not taken notes for the purpose of reporting the cases. Accordingly, while his reports cover the February, 1801; August, 1801; and December, 1801, Terms, *Marbury* v. *Madison* was the first case fully reported by him.

5. Vol. 1, p. 232 (Rev. Ed. 1937).

6. Vol. 3, p. 110 (1919).

7. 1 Cranch at p. 163.

8. *Id.* at p. 170.

9. *Id.* at p. 177.

10. *Id.* at p. 180.

11. Corwin, The Doctrine of Judicial Review, pp. 7-8 (1914).

12. 1 Cranch at p. 299.

PRINCIPAL REFERENCES

1 Warren, The Supreme Court in United States History, 169-316 (Rev. Ed. 1937).

3 Beveridge, The Life of John Marshall, 50-156 (1919).

Corwin, The Doctrine of Judicial Review, 1-80 (1914).

12 Dictionary of American Biography. Article on Marshall by Edward S. Corwin, 319-324 (1933).

Hackett, The Constitutional History of the United States, 1776-1826, 302-309 (1939).

Haines, The Role of the Supreme Court in American Government and Politics, 1789-1835, 223-258 (1944).

III

"Justice the Guardian of Liberty"

JOHN MARSHALL AT THE TRIAL OF AARON BURR*

SHARING SIGNIFICANCE with his rulings was the demeanor of Chief Justice John Marshall throughout the fabulous trial of Aaron Burr in the Circuit Court of the United States in the District of Virginia, March 30-August 31, 1807.

As the presiding trial Justice he exemplified what he meant when he had said for the Supreme Court—

> As there is no crime which can more excite and agitate the passions of men than treason, no charge demands more from the tribunal before which it is made a deliberate and temperate inquiry. Whether this inquiry be directed to the fact or to the law, none can be more solemn, none more important to the citizen or to the government; none can more affect the safety of both.[1]

If ever there was a trial to "excite and agitate the passions of men" it was that of Aaron Burr for high treason. The penalty was death by hanging. The accused was a brilliant lawyer who had served as a Colonel in the Revolutionary Army, United States Senator from New York and Vice President of the United States.[2] Though an Anti-Federalist, he had antagonized the idolized leader of his party, President Jefferson. While Vice President, he had killed, in a duel, the outstanding young leader of the Federalists, Alexander Hamilton. Leaving office in 1805, he was a widely known, ambitious, fearless soldier-statesman to whom fables readily attached themselves. It was rumored that he proposed not only to invade Spanish-held Mexico but to seize New Orleans and sever the Southwest Territories from the United

* Reprinted by permission of the American Bar Association Journal.

States at the Allegheny Mountains. On January 22, 1807, President Jefferson announced to Congress that on these charges Burr's "guilt is placed beyond question."[3] That was enough for the people at large. They denounced Burr as a traitor. They demanded his prompt execution.

The Government, however, faced a new definition of treason in the Constitution of the United States. To convict Burr of treason against the United States in this instance, he must be found guilty of "levying War" against them, and this must be on the testimony of two witnesses to the same overt act. Also, he must be tried by an impartial jury of the state and district wherein the crime was committed. The Government selected as the situs of the crime Blennerhassett's Island in the Ohio River, in Wood County, Virginia, about two miles below the present city of Parkersburg, West Virginia. This brought the trial into the Circuit Court in the District where Chief Justice Marshall would preside as Circuit Justice. The hostility of President Jefferson towards the Chief Justice was well known. That John Marshall did not avoid his responsibility as presiding Justice but discharged it in the deliberate and temperate manner that this *cause célèbre* demanded was in the best tradition of the federal bench.

Today the case is sometimes misconceived. Chief Justice Marshall did not sit alone as presiding Justice. Joining in his rulings and sometimes making comments from the bench was United States District Judge Cyrus Griffin. The rulings of the Circuit Court as to the meaning and required proof of treason were not decisions of first impression in the trial court. In large part they were explanations by the Chief Justice of his own opinion, written for the Supreme Court, February 21, 1807, in *Ex parte Bollman and Swartwout*, 4 Cranch 75, 125. The opinions supporting the principal rulings of the Circuit Court can be found elsewhere than in the often unavailable lower court reports. They were reprinted by Cranch as Appendix B to the Supreme Court opinion just mentioned, at page 470.

The significance of the trial, however, can be fully appreciated only when seen against the background of its time and read in connection with the related litigation.

1. *Background*

On leaving the Vice Presidency Colonel Burr turned to the beckoning fields of adventure in the Southwest. He announced a plan to settle lands he had purchased on the Washita River, in what is now southern Arkansas or northern Louisiana. If the momentarily expected war with Spain developed, he proposed also to lead the first expedition into Mexico. In the event of war, such a procedure on Burr's part apparently would have been welcomed by the United States. In the interest of this project, he visited the Ohio River settlements in 1805 and made plans to meet with his fellow adventurers at or near Blennerhassett's Island in 1806.

Colorful and wild rumors quickly spread about these plans. Over Burr's denials, the rumors included a story that he had conceived a treasonable plan for severing some of the Southwestern Territories from the United States and joining them to a Mexican empire of his own. General James Wilkinson, who commanded the United States Army in the Southwest, but who was at the same time a pensioner of Spain, at first cooperated with Burr. Late in 1806, however, he suddenly reported to President Jefferson that Burr planned to attack New Orleans, seize it and lead a revolt against the United States, all of which Wilkinson proposed to resist by force of arms. It is for historians and not for us to say what degree of truth there was, or that Wilkinson believed there was, in that report.[4]

Burr's alleged treason had remained largely in the realm of rumor until General Wilkinson wrote to the President. Relying on Wilkinson, the President submitted the issue to his Cabinet and, on November 27, 1806, sent Congress a proclamation that startled the nation. It reported receipt of information that a military expedition was being organized by private persons within the United States to move against the dominions of Spain, and that such persons were collecting arms and seducing well-meaning citizens "to engage in their criminal enterprises." The President warned faithful citizens to withdraw from the enterprise or "incur prosecution with all the rigors of the law." He enjoined civil and military officers to seize the boats, arms, etc., so provided. He required good and faithful citizens to aid in "bringing to justice" all such offenders and in "giving information against them to the proper authorities."[5] The proclamation did not name anyone as the offender nor specifically charge anyone with treason against the United States. The public, however, knew that Burr was the alleged offender and jumped to the conclusion that he must be guilty of high treason or the President would not have taken such extraordinary steps to thwart his preparations. The proclamation apparently had two effects. As the President later claimed, it probably destroyed all likelihood of the success of any such treasonable plans against the United States as were reported by Wilkinson. It also convinced the public that Burr had undertaken such plans as were described. Throughout his life Burr suffered the consequences of that popular belief.

On December 2, 1806, the President, in his annual message, reminded Congress of the reported expedition of private individuals against the territories of Spain.[6] Congress demanded that the President disclose his information concerning such a conspiracy and report the measures he had taken to suppress it. He replied that his information was voluminous but that there was little in it to constitute legal evidence. He, however, detailed General Wilkinson's report of Burr's alleged treason and misdemeanor, referred to his own proclamation of November 27, 1806, identified Burr as the principal actor, and assured Congress that *Burr's "guilt is placed beyond question."*[7] The die was cast. The prosecution of Burr for treason became politically necessary. The unflinching adherence of the courts to their impartial duties under these circumstances deserves recognition. As the Chief Justice later said of his Circuit Court: "That this court dares not usurp power is most true. That this court dares not shrink from its duty is not less true."[8]

A summary of the related litigation will outline the ensuing drama.[9]

2. *Proceedings Before Those in Richmond*

A. *November, 1806—In the Circuit Court of the United States in the District of Kentucky* (Innis, J.). A federal indictment was sought in Kentucky against Burr for the misdemeanor of preparing a military expedition within the United States against Spain. He appeared voluntarily and the investigation collapsed.[10]

B. *December, 1806—In the same court.* Similar indictments were sought against Burr and Adair. Burr appeared voluntarily and was represented by Henry Clay. The grand jury, after hearing the evidence, not only refused to indict Burr but rendered a special report, finding that they could not "discover that anything improper or injurious to the interest of the Government of the United States, or contrary to the laws thereof, is designed or contemplated by either of them [Burr or Adair]."[11]

C. *December, 1806-January, 1807. In New Orleans.* This constituted most of General Wilkinson's "reign of terror." When the Governor refused the General's request to suspend the writ of habeas corpus or to declare martial law, the General seized local military control in the name of national security. He arrested and shipped to Baltimore Bollman, Swartwout, Alexander, and later Adair. He also seized others. Writs of habeas corpus were issued by local judges.

[46]

To these the General made returns that he took full responsibility for the arrests and stated that the men sought were no longer in his possession. Judge Workman appealed to the Governor for help. Receiving none, he adjourned his court and shortly thereafter resigned his office.[12] At the request of the General, the Governor asked the Territorial Legislature to suspend the writ of habeas corpus. The Legislature not only refused but forwarded to Congress a memorial of protest.[13]

D. *December, 1806-January, 1807. Progress of Burr's expedition.* The immediate prospect of war with Spain having been dissipated, Burr, Blennerhassett, Tyler, and Smith floated down the Mississippi River with nine flatboats, manned by about six men each. They proposed to settle on the Washita. At the same time the rumor spread that Burr was coming to attack New Orleans with hundreds or thousands of men, and General Wilkinson mobilized his forces to intercept them.

On December 2 Governor Tiffin of Ohio, aroused by a representative from the President, sent a warning message to the Ohio Legislature. This led to the seizure, on December 9, of some of Blennerhassett's unmanned flatboats on the Muskingum River in Ohio. On December 10 the Virginia militia announced that it would investigate Blennerhassett's Island on the following day. The expedition, being substantially ready to leave, created further excitement by leaving during the night. The next day the militia ransacked the island, consumed the liquid spirits available, and seized a flatboat with fourteen boys from Pittsburgh aboard. The prisoners were released after brief questioning and, taking Mrs. Blennerhassett with them, proceeded down the river.

On December 22 Colonel Burr joined the party at the mouth of the Cumberland with two boats which had been prepared for him by General Andrew Jackson. Passing down the Mississippi on Christmas Day, he dispatched a friendly note to the Commander at Fort Massac. On December 29 Burr declined an equally friendly invitation to dine at the Fort. There was nothing about Burr's little flotilla to cause alarm to those who saw it. Nevertheless, intense excitement had been aroused in the Mississippi Territory by exaggerated warnings of its approach. A detachment of 375 militiamen was sent up the river to intercept it. Other troops marched by land. On their contact with Burr, he ridiculed the idea of his hostility and volunteered to submit to the civil authorities. The inflated monster of impending military invasion collapsed.[14] At the town of Washington in the Territory of Mississippi, Burr was bound over to await action of the grand jury. General Wilkinson boasted that he had dissipated the conspiracy and had saved New Orleans.

E. *February, 1807. In the Supreme Court of the Mississippi Territory*. Burr volunteered to answer any bill of indictment. The District Attorney, after examination of the depositions submitted to him, asked the court to discharge the grand jury. The court refused, whereupon the grand jury filed a report favorable to Burr and condemnatory of his accusers. The forthrightness of this frontier document is refreshing.[15] Although no indictment was found against Burr, he bound over to appear from day to day. At the same time a military patrol was on its way from General Wilkinson who had pledged $5,000 to cover the expenses of Burr's capture. Fearing for his life, Burr went into hiding and notified the Governor that he would submit to civil law when assured of the rights of a citizen. Attempting to flee the Territory, Burr was recognized by one Perkins and was reported to a lieutenant who arrested him. Perkins received $3,331.

F. *January-February, 1807. In Washington*. In Jefferson's response to the House of Representatives of January 22 he had stated that Burr's conspiracy contemplated two objects—the severance of the Union and an attack on Mexico. The next day the Senate, in closed session, on motion of Senator Giles of Virginia, passed a bill to suspend the writ of habeas corpus. In contrast, the House, in open session, rejected the bill 113 to 19. Going further the House almost passed, 58 to 60, what would have amounted to a vote of censure of the Administration.

At this moment, Wilkinson's military prisoners began to arrive in Washington from New Orleans. Jefferson ordered them delivered to the civil authorities and General Wilkinson's evidence presented to the courts. Alexander was promptly released by Judge Duchet for lack of competent evidence against him. Bollman and Swartwout, having been committed to jail by the Circuit Court for the District of Columbia, sought, on February 13, a writ of habeas corpus directly from the Supreme Court of the United States which was then in session. Bollman and Swartwout also sought a writ of certiorari to bring up the record of their commitment. Both writs were allowed and motions to discharge the prisoners were argued February 16, 17 and 18. Counsel appearing for the prisoners included former United States Attorney General Charles Lee, Francis Scott Key, later to become the author of our national anthem, and Luther Martin, a leader of the Maryland and American Bars. Of the Court there were present Chief Justice Marshall and Justices Chase, Washington and William Johnson. Justices Cushing and Livingston were absent.[16] The evidence presented by the prosecution was reviewed in detail by the Court.[17] On February 21, Chief Justice Marshall announced the opinion of the Court, discharging the prisoners for lack of the proof necessary to constitute treason by levying war against the United States.[18]

General Adair and Ogden were landed in Baltimore where Judge Nicholson released them, reporting to the President that "very much to my surprise and mortification . . . there was no proof of any nature whatsoever with them."[19] Adair

[49]

later sued General Wilkinson, in Natchez, for false imprisonment. After eight years, he recovered $2,500 damages, which the Government paid.

3. *Preliminary Proceedings in Richmond*

The Government next concentrated upon the prosecution of Burr for treason. A determined effort was made to gather evidence by widespread use of printed questionnaires. Since the Circuit Court in the District of Virginia was selected for the trial, it was necessary to find accommodations for the public at the hearings. As a result the court sat in the hall of the House of Delegates of the Commonwealth of Virginia from March into September, 1807.

A. *Counsel.* Government counsel was led by District Attorney George Hay, son-in-law of the future President, James Monroe. Hay was in personal correspondence with President Jefferson on every important point of policy. With Hay was William Wirt, then 35. He was destined to become a distinguished author and to serve as Attorney General under Presidents Monroe and John Quincy Adams. Supplementing these was Alexander MacRae, Lieutenant Governor of Virginia. Counsel for the accused served without compensation. They included Edmund Randolph, former Attorney General under President Washington; John Wickham, a leader of the Virginia Bar; Luther Martin, for many years Attorney General of Maryland, and recognized nationally as a learned and effective trial lawyer; Charles Lee, former Attorney General under Presidents Washington and John Adams; and as junior counsel Benjamin Botts and John Baker. Burr himself often took part in the examinations of witnesses and in arguments to the court. Unlike most lawyers, he was his own best advocate.

B. *March 30, 1807.* Shortly after Burr's arrival in Richmond under military guard, Chief Justice Marshall himself wrote out, signed and issued the warrant by virtue of which Burr was surrendered to the civil authorities.

c. *March 30-April 1, 1807. Commitment.* Relying on the record in the *Bollman* and *Swartwout* cases, the prosecution asked the Chief Justice to commit Burr to jail on two charges: treason against the United States and misdemeanor in preparing and setting on foot within the United States a military expedition against Spain. After reviewing the evidence, the Chief Justice held it not sufficient to sustain commitment for treason but sufficient to sustain commitment for the misdemeanor.[20] He ordered Burr committed on that charge, but released him on $10,000 bail, conditioned on his appearance at the next term of court, May 22.

d. *May 22, 1807. The grand jury.* The required sixteen, out of a panel of twenty-four, were present and available for service on the grand jury. Burr, however, personally challenged "for favour" U. S. Senator Giles of Virginia, and Colonel Nicholas, a candidate for Congress, both of whom were strong partisans of Jefferson. Burr's objection to Senator Giles included the latter's recent effort in the Senate to suspend the writ of habeas corpus, indicating substantial belief in the reports to Congress on Burr's expedition. Burr offered to prove that the Senator had confirmed such beliefs by public declarations. Burr objected to Colonel Nicholas on the ground that the latter entertained a bitter personal animosity towards him. Both of those challenged withdrew from the panel. The sixteen finally accepted included some of the foremost citizens of Virginia. Two were Federalists, fourteen were Anti-Federalists. The Chief Justice named as foreman John Randolph, an Anti-Jeffersonian. In instructing the grand jury, Chief Justice Marshall followed the opinion he had written for the Supreme Court in *Ex parte Bollman and Swartwout, supra.*[21]

e. *May 22-28, 1807. Second motion to commit Burr for treason.* The District Attorney announced in open court that he would again move to commit Burr to jail on the charge of treason, arguing that, with the approach of General Wilkinson and the Government's principal witnesses, there was increased danger that Burr might not remain available. This motion had the earmarks of propaganda but the court ruled that if the District Attorney had something to present in support of such a motion, he had a right to do so.[22] Witnesses were called as to the activities of Burr and his associates at Blennerhassett's Island. Collateral issues arose as to the admissibility of certain affidavits and as to their certification. The court ruled against their admissibility.[23] The Chief Justice indicated that he hoped that no opinion would be required of him on this motion to commit for treason, prior to some action by the grand jury. When Burr agreed to double his bond, the motion was abandoned.

F. *June 9-13, 1807. The subpoena to the President.* Burr moved for issuance of a *subpoena duces tecum* directed to President Jefferson personally, calling upon him to produce a certain letter from General Wilkinson deemed material to the defense. After bitter argument, the court ordered the subpoena to be issued. The Chief Justice stated that, while this was the court's inescapable duty, it remained for the President to indicate in the return whether his executive duties would constitute a sufficient reason for not obeying it.[24] This issue never reached its climax. The District Attorney later announced that he had the requested letter in his possession and was ready to produce it.

G. *June 15-18, 1807. Immunity of witnesses on ground of self-incrimination.* An issue arose as to the extent to which the court could go in requiring the secretary to Colonel Burr to state whether he, the secretary, understood the cipher letter which he had written for Colonel Burr. He declined to answer on the ground that his answer might tend to incriminate him. This resulted in a ruling that the witness could answer whether he *presently* understood the cipher, without its tending to incriminate him. The opinion states the views of the Chief Justice on the rules applicable to such cases.[25]

H. *June 19-27, 1807. Attachment of General Wilkinson was sought* by Burr's counsel for Wilkinson's alleged contempt of court and abuse of power in his efforts to induce witnesses to testify for the Government. The argument on this motion was interrupted by the grand jury's return of the indictments. The following day, the motion was denied.[26]

I. *June 26, 1807. The indictments.* After extended hearings, the grand jury indicted both Burr and Blennerhassett not only for the misdemeanor charged but also for treason. The indictments for treason charged that on December 10, 1806, at Blennerhassett's Island, the accused had levied war against the United States by the assembly there of a "multitude" of thirty or more people, armed and arrayed in a warlike and hostile manner.[27] The other indictments alleged that at the same place the accused had set on foot an armed expedition against territory of the King of Spain. Two days later the grand jury returned similar indictments against United States Senator Smith of Ohio, former United States Senator Dayton of New Jersey, Tyler, Israel Smith and Floyd. Seven jurors voted to indict General Wilkinson but nine voted not to do so. Bollman, Swartwout and Adair were not indicted.

3. *The Trial*

A. *June 26-27, 1807. Burr pleaded not guilty to the indictment for treason.* The court ordered that, inasmuch as the trial could not, without great inconvenience, be held in Wood County where the offense was alleged to have been committed, the marshal should summon forty-eight "fit persons," twelve of whom should be from Wood County, to appear in Richmond on August 3, 1807, as a jury panel. From this time until the end of the trial, Burr remained committed in specially provided quarters.

B. *August 3-17, 1807. Impaneling the jury.* Out of the forty-eight persons summoned, only four were accepted as petit jurors and only one of those expressed himself as being entirely unprejudiced. After making a careful statement as to the proper qualification of jurors, the court ordered another panel of forty-eight.[28] The result of their examination was no better. Finally, the accused suggested that he select jurors from those who had expressed hostility to him but to whom nevertheless he would be willing to submit his case. This implied strong faith by the accused, both in his innocence and in the fairness of the jury. It was a bold step in a capital case where there was such a popular demand for conviction. Among the jurors so chosen was one who testified that he had said that Burr should be hanged and another who had said "in the utmost spirit of levity" that he had come to Richmond with the hope of being chosen on the jury where, if accepted, he would vote to hang the defendant at once without further inquiry.[29]

C. *August 17-18, 1807. Order of proof.* Upon the appearance of General Eaton as the prosecution's first witness, proof of Burr's hostile intentions in performing the particular overt acts charged in the indictment was objected to by Burr's counsel unless preceded by proof of the overt acts themselves. The court overruled the objection. It indicated that both the overt act and the hostile intent accompanying it were material to the proof of levying war, and that the court should not prescribe which of the two material elements the prosecution must present first. The court added, however, that testimony relating to any plans of Burr's which, for example, were to be executed in Washington or elsewhere than in the District of Virginia, would not be an element of the particular treason charged in the indictment. While such testimony might later become admissible as corroborative of Burr's general evil intentions and thus "render it more probable that the intention in the particular case was

[54]

evil," it would become admissible only "after hearing that which it is to confirm." The testimony of General Eaton thus was permitted to be given insofar as it related directly to the overt acts charged and the hostile intent of the accused accompanying them.[30]

D. *August 18-31, 1807. The crucial lack of proof.* By August 20 the Government had not presented testimony of the presence or other actual participation of Burr in the assemblage at Blennerhassett's Island. On the contrary the evidence showed Burr's absence and his failure to participate in the assemblage. The defense accordingly objected to the introduction of any further evidence. In the absence of the constitutionally required testimony of the overt act of treason charged in the indictment, they contended that all other evidence would be immaterial. The Government recognized the propriety of the procedure. It argued, however, for permission to show that the accused had advised and procured the assemblage and that the assemblage constituted levying war against the United States.

After ten days of able argument,[13] the Chief Justice, on August 31, delivered the final opinion in the case.[32] He took occasion to explain and amplify the opinion he had written for the Supreme Court in *Ex parte Bollman and Swartwout*, 4 Cranch 75, 125. While it was not essential to the decision here, he indicated it to be his personal view that the constitutional requirement of levying war against the United States would be satisfied by finding the fact to be that there had been gathered at Blennerhassett's Island a military assemblage in force, with a warlike intent towards the United States and in condition to make such war. He indicated further that the evidence already before the court would justify its submission to the jury on that point, provided there were also before the court the required testimony as to the accused's participation in the assemblage.

He discussed the alleged activity of the accused in advising and procuring the assemblage. He pointed out that there had not yet been presented two witnesses to overt acts showing such advice or procurement. While not passing finally upon the point, he indicated that, to be admissible as overt acts of treason, such acts of advice or procurement should be charged in an indictment laid in the state and district where the trial would be held. No such acts of advice or procurement having been charged in the instant case, they could not be substituted for those which had been charged. Their admissibility as mere corroboration of other testimony was impossible in the absence of testimony to be corroborated.

In short, the prosecution had failed to meet the constitutional requirement that the guilt of the accused be established by the testimony of two witnesses to the same overt act of the accused in levying war at a specified time and place within the jurisdiction of the trial court. The Chief Justice concluded:

> No testimony relative to the conduct or declarations of the prisoner elsewhere, and subsequent to the transaction on Blennerhassett's Island, can be admitted; because such testimony, being in its nature merely corroborative and incompetent to prove the overt act in itself, is irrelevant until there be proof of the overt act by two witnesses. This opinion does not comprehend the proof by two witnesses that the meeting on Blennerhassett's Island was procured by the prisoner. On that point the court for the present withholds its opinion for reasons which have been already assigned; and as it is understood from the statements made on the part of the prosecution that no such testimony exists, if there be such let it be offered, and the court will decide upon it.
>
> The jury have now heard the opinion of the court on the law of the case. They will apply that law to the facts, and will find a verdict of guilty or not guilty as their own consciences may direct.[33]

The court granted the prosecution's request to consider the court's opinion overnight. The next morning the prosecutor informed the court that he had nothing to offer to the jury, either in the way of evidence or argument. The jury retired and in a short time returned with the following verdict, prepared in a form of their origination: "We of the jury say that Aaron Burr is not proved to be guilty under this indictment by any evidence submitted to us. We therefore find him not guilty."[34]

The trial was over. The nation had reason to feel that, when administered after the manner of Marshall, Justice is the Guardian of Liberty.[35]

NOTES TO CHAPTER III

1. *Ex parte Bollman and Swartwout,* 4 Cranch 75, 125.

2. He had presided in the Senate, with marked fairness and competency, over the impeachment trial of Associate Justice Chase of the Supreme Court which had resulted in an acquittal of the Justice. January 2-March 1, 1805. See Annals, 8th Cong., 2d Sess. 80-675, 726-763. On leaving the Vice Presidency, he had delivered to the Senate, in executive session, March 2, 1805, an affecting farewell address marked with expressions of strong devotion to his country and its Constitution. Annals, 8th Cong., 2d Sess. 71-72.

3. President's Message to Congress, Annals, 9th Cong., 2d Sess. 39-43.

4. Andrew Jackson supported Burr's settlement program and refused to believe the charges of treason. He helped Burr outfit his river boats and entertained him at his home. When ordered to mobilize his militia in defense against Burr's supposedly revolutionary movements, he did so. After reinvestigating the facts, he promptly disbanded his militia. In McCaleb's "The Aaron Burr Conspiracy" he is quoted as writing the following confidential letter, January 15, 1807:

"The late denunciation of Aaron Burr as a traitor has excited great surprise and general indignation against Burr. Still, from the opinion possessed of the accuser (Wilkinson) many there are who wait for the proof before they will pronounce him guilty of the charge. . . . And if Burr had any treasonable intentions in view, he is the basest of all human beings. I will tell you why. He always held out the idea of settling Washita, unless a war with Spain; in that event he held out the idea that from his intimacy with the Secretary of War, he would obtain an appointment; and if he did he would revolutionize Mexico. . . . If he is a traitor, he is the basest that ever did commit treason, and being tore to pieces and scattered to the four winds of heaven would be too good for him." At p. 218.

[57]

During Burr's trial, Jackson was summoned to Richmond as a State witness but he so vigorously denounced Wilkinson and supported Burr that he was not put on the stand. He wrote from Richmond before the trial was well begun: "I am more convinced than ever that treason was never intended by Burr; but if it was, you know my wishes—that he may be hung. I am still more convinced that whatever may have been the project of Burr, James Wilkinson has gone hand and hand with him." *Id.* at p. 219.

McCaleb quotes, as "the most explicit enunciation we have of his [Burr's] concerning the nature of the project," the following language apparently used in a communication from Burr to Senator John Smith of Ohio:

"Mr. Smith, my object in a few months will be disclosed; you will not find it dishonorable or inimical to this Government. I feel superior to the mean artifices which are ascribed to me. Calumniators I do not notice, for as fast as you put one down another will rise up. This much I will tell you: if there should be a war between the United States and Spain, I shall head a corps of volunteers and be the first to march into the Mexican provinces. If peace should be proffered, which I do not expect, I shall settle my Washita lands, and make society as pleasant as possible. In this Government I have been persecuted, shamefully persecuted; and I am sorry to say, that in it, all private confidence is destroyed." *Id.* at p. 156, citing Liberty Hall (a Cincinnati newspaper), February 24, 1807.

Similarly, when Henry Clay was representing Burr before the Federal Circuit Court in Kentucky, Burr, on December 1, 1806, categorically denied to Clay the rumors then in circulation saying:

"I have no design, nor have I taken any measure, to promote a dissolution of the Union or a separation of any one or more States from the residue. . . . I do not own a musket nor a bayonet, nor any single article of military stores, nor does any person for me, by my authority or with my knowledge. . . . Considering the high station you now fill in our national councils [United States Senator from Kentucky], I have thought these explanations proper, as well to counteract the chimerical tales, which malevolent persons have so industriously circulated, as to satisfy you that you have not espoused the cause of a man in any way unfriendly to the laws, the government, or the interests of his country." *Id.* at p. 157.

5. Proclamation Against Burr's Plot, 10 Ford, The Works of Thomas Jefferson, 301-302.

6. Annals, 9th Cong., 2d Sess. 11, 12.

7. "In this state of the evidence, delivered sometimes too under the restriction of private confidence, neither safety nor justice will permit the exposing names, except that of the principal actor [Burr], whose guilt is placed beyond question." Jefferson's Message to Congress, January 22, 1807, Annals, 9th Cong., 2d Sess. 39, 40.

8. *United States* v. *Burr*, 25 Fed. Cas., No. 14,693, p. 179, also in App. B, 4 Cranch at p. 506.

9. The record of the proceedings is largely available in:
(1). Robertson's Reports of the Trials of Colonel Aaron Burr (1808), cited by McCaleb as Burr's Trials. This is a two-volume publication con-

taining, in 1135 pages, a substantially complete transcript of the record in the prosecutions, both for treason and misdemeanors in the Circuit Court of the United States, at Richmond, Virginia, taken in shorthand by David Robertson. See also, Coombs, The Trial of Aaron Burr for High Treason, condensed to 390 pages, largely omitting arguments of counsel.

(2). *United States* v. *Burr*, 25 Fed. Cas., Nos. 14,692, 14,692a, 14,692b, 14,692c, 14,692d, 14,692e, 14,692f, 14,692g, 14,692h, 14,693, 14,694, 14,694a, at pp. 1-207. These contain the opinions in the several related cases. Those in the principal proceeding are in No. 14,693 and Marshall's major opinion of August 31, 1807, is at pp. 159-181.

(3). *Ex parte Bollman and Swartwout*, 4 Cranch 75. This contains the opinions delivered in the Supreme Court in February, 1807, on several of the underlying issues which arose again in Burr's trial. As Appendix A, at pp. 455-470, there are reprinted the documents which accompanied the President's message of January 22, 1807. As Appendix B, at pp. 471-507, there is reprinted the opinion rendered by Chief Justice Marshall, as Circuit Justice for the Circuit Court in the District of Virginia, August 31, 1807. The reporter states, at p. 125 note, that the opinion in the Circuit Court "elucidates and explains some passages in this opinion [of the Supreme Court in the *Bollman* case] which were supposed to be in some degree doubtful."

10. *United States* v. *Burr*, 25 Fed. Cas., No. 14,692, pp. 1-2.

11. McCaleb, The Aaron Burr Conspiracy, p. 163, citing Paladium, December 11, 1806.

12. The General soon seized this judge and another man, charging both with planning or participating in expeditions against Spanish possessions. Each was found not guilty when tried in March, 1808.

13. ". . . no foreign enemy or open domestic foe was then, or has yet been proved to have been within any perilous distance of this city. . . . The acts of high-handed military power to which we have been exposed [are] too notorious to be denied, too illegal to be justified, too wanton to be excused." McCaleb, The Aaron Burr Conspiracy, p. 198, citing Orleans Gazette, Extra, March 20, 1807.

14. Cowles Meade, the acting Governor of the Mississippi Territory, reported to the Government as follows:
". . . this mighty alarm, with all its exaggeration, has eventuated in nine boats and one hundred men, and the major part of these are boys, or young men just from school. Many of their depositions have been taken before Judge Rodney, but they bespeak ignorance of the views or designs of the Colonel. I believe them really ignorant and deluded. I believe that they are really the dupes of stratagem, if the asservations of Generals Eaton and Wilkinson are to be accredited." McCaleb, The Aaron Burr Conspiracy, p. 225.

15. "The grand jury of the Mississippi Territory, on a due investigation of the evidence brought before them, are of the opinion that Aaron Burr has not been guilty of any crime or misdemeanor against the laws of the United States or of this Territory, or given any just occasion for alarm or inquietude to the good people of this Territory. The grand jury present as

a grievance, the late military expedition unnecessarily as they conceive, fitted out against the person and property of said Aaron Burr, where no resistance has been made to the ordinary civil authorities. The grand jury also present as highly derogatory to the dignity of this Government, the armistice (so-called) concluded between the Secretary, acting as Governor, and the said Aaron Burr. The grand jury also present as a grievance, destructive of personal liberty, the late military arrests made without warrant, and as they conceive, without other lawful authority: and they do seriously regret that so much cause should be given to the enemies of our glorious Constitution, to rejoice in such measures being adopted in a neighboring Territory, and if sanctioned by the Executive of our country, must sap the vitals of our political existence, and crumble this glorious fabric into the dust." McCaleb, The Aaron Burr Conspiracy, p. 228, citing Orleans Gazette, February 20, 1807.

16. Justices Cushing and Chase were appointees of President Washington, Justice Bushrod Washington and Chief Justice Marshall of President John Adams, and Justices William Johnson and Brockholst Livingston of President Jefferson. Justice Todd was added to the Court March 3, 1807, by President Jefferson. It appears that the Chief Justice later communicated individually with the members of the Supreme Court at some time before his Circuit Court's hearing of the *Burr* case, beginning August 3, 1807. 3 Beveridge, The Life of John Marshall, 480-481, and references made by the Chief Justice to the individual views of some of the Justices, expressed subsequent to the decision in the *Bollman* case. See *United States* v. *Burr*, 25 Fed. Cas., No. 14,693, at p. 161, s. c., App. B, 4 Cranch at pp. 474-475.

17. See 4 Cranch, App. A, pp. 455-469.

18. *Ex parte Bollman and Swartwout*, 4 Cranch 75, 125.

19. McCaleb, The Aaron Burr Conspiracy, p. 249, citing Nicholson to Jefferson, February 18, 1807.

20. *United States* v. *Burr*, 25 Fed. Cas., No. 14,692a, pp. 2-25.

21. See 3 Beveridge, The Life of John Marshall, 350, 414 n., 466, 484, 506; 1 Robertson's Reports of the Trials of Colonel Aaron Burr, pp. 31-46.

22. 25 Fed. Cas., No. 14,692b, pp. 25-27.

23. 25 Fed. Cas., No. 14,692c, pp. 27-30.

24. 25 Fed. Cas., No. 14,692d, pp. 30-38.

25. 25 Fed. Cas., No. 14,692e, pp. 38-41.
"The gentlemen of the bar will understand the rule laid down by the court to be this: It is the province of the court to judge whether any direct answer to the question which may be proposed will furnish evidence against the witness. If such answer may disclose a fact which forms a necessary and essential link in the chain of testimony, which would be sufficient to convict him of any crime, he is not bound to answer it so as to furnish matter for that conviction. In such a case the witness must himself judge what his answer will be; and if he say on oath that he cannot answer without accusing himself, he cannot be compelled to answer." *Id.*, pp. 40-41.

26. 25 Fed. Cas., No. 14,692f, pp. 41-49.

27. "The grand inquest of the United States of America, for the Virginia district, upon their oath, do present, that Aaron Burr . . . owing allegiance and fidelity to the same United States, not having the fear of God before his eyes, nor weighing the duty of his said allegiance, but being moved and seduced by the instigation of the devil, wickedly devising and intending the peace and tranquillity of the said United States to disturb; and to stir, move and excite insurrection, rebellion and war against the said United States; on the tenth day of December, in the year of Christ one thousand eight hundred and six, at a certain place called and known by the name of Blannerhassett's (*sic*) island . . . did compass, imagine and intend to raise and levy war, insurrection and rebellion against the said United States; and in order to fulfil and bring to effect the said traitorous compassings, imaginations and intentions of him the said Aaron Burr . . . with a great multitude of persons, whose names at present are unknown to the grand inquest aforesaid, to a great number, to wit, to the number of thirty persons and upwards, armed and arrayed in a warlike manner, that is to say, with guns, swords, and dirks, and other warlike weapons as well offensive as defensive, being then and there unlawfully, maliciously and traitorously assembled and gathered together, did falsely and traitorously assemble and join themselves together against the said United States; . . . ." 1 Robertson's Reports of the Trials of Colonel Aaron Burr, pp. 430-431.

28. 25 Fed. Cas., No. 14,692g, pp. 49-52.

29. "MILES BOTT. From the affidavits of Generals Wilkinson and Eaton, my opinion has been completely made up for several months past.

"MR. MARTIN—I suppose you have only taken up a prejudice on the supposition, that the facts stated were true.

"MR. BOTT. I have gone so far as to declare, that Colonel Burr ought to be hanged.

"MR. BURR.—Do you think that such declarations would now influence your judgment? Would not the evidence alter your opinion?

"ANSWER. Human nature is very frail; I know that the evidence ought, but it might or might not influence me. I have expressed myself in this manner, perhaps, within a fortnight; and I do not consider myself a proper juryman.

"MR. BURR.—It will be seen, either that I am under the necessity of taking men in some degree, prejudiced against me, or of having another venire. I am unwilling to submit to the further delay of other '*tales*,' and I must therefore encounter the consequences. I will take Mr. Bott, under the belief that he will do me justice." 1 Robertson's Reports of the Trials of Colonel Aaron Burr, p. 426

See also, examination of Christoper Anthony at pp. 423-425

30. 25 Fed. Cas., No. 14,692h, pp. 52-54.

31. The Chief Justice paid tribute to this argument as follows:

"The question now to be decided has been argued in a manner worthy of its importance, and with an earnestness evincing the strong conviction felt by the counsel on each side that the law is with them. A degree of eloquence seldom displayed on any occasion has embellished a solidity of argument and a depth of research by which the court has been greatly aided in forming the opinion it is about to deliver." 25 Fed. Cas., No. 14,693, at p. 159, s. c., 4 Cranch at p. 470.

One eloquent passage from the argument of William Wirt on August 25, against treating Blennerhassett as the principal and Burr as an accessory, was printed for many years thereafter in school books for use as a declamation. 25 Fed. Cas., No. 14,693, at pp. 131-132. It is quoted, in part, in 3 Beveridge, The Life of John Marshall, 616-618, and, together with Benjamin Bott's deflating response, is discussed at pp. 495-500.

32. 25 Fed. Cas., No. 14,693, pp. 55-186, at pp. 159-181.

33. *Id.*, p. 180.

34. Burr at once objected to the form of this "not-proven" or "Scotch Verdict" in place of a simple one of "not guilty." The Chief Justice replied that the verdict was, in effect, the same as a verdict of acquittal, that it should remain as found by the jury, and that an entry be made on the record of "not guilty." Hill, Decisive Battles of the Law, 62.

As in each of the related proceedings, the necessary proof to sustain the charges had been found lacking when put to the final test. Thus acquitted of treason, Burr was then tried on the indictment for the misdemeanor. He was acquitted on September 14, 1807. 25 Fed. Cas., No. 14,694, pp. 187-201. The Government dropped its prosecutions of most of his associates. A district attorney, however, sought further commitments of Burr and Blennerhassett for trial in the Mississippi Territory and in Ohio. Commitments for treason were denied. Commitments for misdemeanors in Ohio were ordered and bail was posted, but the accused apparently were never indicted.

35. "Justice the Guardian of Liberty" is the inscription on the East Portico of the Supreme Court Building in Washington. It is a modification of one proposed by the architect. It was put in its present form by Chief Justice Hughes in consultation with Justice Van Devanter, Chairman and member, respectively, of the Supreme Court Building Commission. It is less well known than that on the West Portico, over the entrance to the building—"Equal Justice Under Law." The latter was approved by Chief Justice Hughes and Justice Van Devanter in precisely the form in which it was submitted to them. Neither inscription is a direct quotation from any identified source.

PRINCIPAL REFERENCES

Ex parte Bollman and Swartwout, 4 Cranch 75-137, 455-507.

Cramer v. *United States,* 325 U. S. 1.

Haupt v. *United States,* 330 U. S. 631.

United States v. *Burr,* 25 Fed. Cas., Nos. 14,692-14,694a, pp. 1-207.

1 and 2 Robertson, Reports of the Trials of Colonel Aaron Burr (1808).

Hurst, Treason in the United States, 58 Harv. L. Rev. 226-272, 395-444, 806-846 (1944-1945).

McCaleb, The Aaron Burr Conspiracy (1936).

3 Beveridge, The Life of John Marshall, 274-545 (1919).

Jenkinson, Aaron Burr (1902).

Hill, Decisive Battles of the Law, 27-64 (1907).

Cabell, The Trial of Aaron Burr, 23 Proceedings N. Y. State Bar Assn. 56-86 (1900).

IV

The Story of the Place

PLACES, LIKE PEOPLE, have personalities. They also have careers. The site of the Supreme Court Building in Washington is as rich in historical interest as it is now radiant in architectural symmetry. Its colorful career falls into nine contrasting periods.

1. Before 1790 Came Centuries of Serenity

Let us begin with Capitol Hill as it was in 1550 and as it had been for centuries before that. No human being other than an occasional Indian had seen "The Hill," much less visited its crest at sundown and from there watched the sun set across the still waters and the blue ridge to the west. The hilltop was covered with oak trees. The marshy land below it was filled with sycamores, silver poplars and alders. From the north, a nameless brook wound its way through the woods and westerly to the river. To the south another brook bubbled from a spring. The tourists of that day were the deer, the bears, the raccoons and the wild turkeys. The permanent residents were the grey squirrels—predecessors of those that today enjoy their prescriptive rights to the hollow tree trunks on the Capitol Plaza. "The Hill" of that day was known only to the animals, to the Indians, and to God. It was a quiet place that lent itself to inspiration.

By 1650 a trail had been blazed from the settlements in the

* Written in cooperation with Thomas E. Waggaman, then Marshal of the Supreme Court of the United States, and reprinted by permission of The George Washington Law Review.

north to the Indian Village near the falls of the Potomac. Captain John Smith and others, paddling up from the south, had reached those falls by canoe. Lord Baltimore had claimed the area under a proprietary grant from Charles I of England. It was all in a province named Maryland, in honor of Queen Henrietta Maria.

In another hundred years commerce had begun to flow from the trading center at Bladensburg to Georgetown and thence to Alexandria. Title to the land was vested in private ownership. Some of the properties were known as manors. They produced tobacco and corn. Before 1790 the manor which included "The Hill" had been inherited by Daniel Carroll of Duddington. It extended approximately from what today is L Street on the north of the Capitol to N Street on the south, between Third Street on the west, and Third Street on the east.[1] The brook that flowed from the north across the foot of the hill had been named Goose Creek. Later it was to be renamed Tiber Creek and flow into the canal where now we see Constitution Avenue. The brook that bubbled down to the Anacostia River had been named St. James Creek. Later it was destined to be the St. James Canal. "The Hill" was in the very center of this Carroll property. It was known as Jenkins Hill and no one dreamed that it might become a point of interest to the world.

2. *1790-1815 Brought the District of Columbia to "The Hill"*

Late in 1788 the new Constitution for the United States of America gave the world a new guaranty of freedom. In it was Article I, §8, pregnant with destiny for "The Hill." That clause gave Congress power to "exercise exclusive Legislation . . . over such District (not exceeding ten miles square) as may, by Cession of particular States, and the Acceptance of Congress, become the Seat of the Government of the United States. . . ." In 1790, such a District, ten miles square, centered around "The Hill," was recommended by President Washington and his adviser, Major Charles Pierre L'Enfant, as the seat of that new Government. Promptly Maryland, Virginia, and the Congress concurred. The hand of history wrote fast. In 1791 a cornerstone of the District was laid in what is now Alexandria, Virginia. The diagonal axis of the square extending due north located about one-third of the District west of the Potomac in Virginia and two-thirds of it east of the Potomac in Maryland. The President named three Commissioners for its government. They were David Stuart of Virginia, Daniel Carroll of Maryland, and Thomas Johnson, also of Maryland. Carroll had been a member of the Constitutional Convention of 1787. He was not, however, the Daniel Carroll of Duddington who owned Jenkins Hill. Thomas Johnson had been a member of the Continental Congress and the first Governor of Maryland. Later he was to sit as an Associate Justice on the Supreme Court of the United States.

In 1791 they named this District of Destiny the "Territory of Columbia" and that part of the District which lay west of the Potomac soon was ceded back to Virginia. The remaining two-thirds is the "District of Columbia" as we know it today. The Commissioners required a small area within the District to be laid out in streets and squares. They named that area the "City of Washington." Its streets, running due east and west, were to be lettered alphabetically, in two series, to the north and south from the Capitol Grounds. Similarly, those running due north and south were to be numbered consecutively, in two series, to the east and west from the same point. Major L'Enfant located the site for the Nation's Capitol on Jenkins Hill. On the same map he located First Street, N. E. Likewise he identified, as Square No. 728, the area on First Street extending north from East Capitol Street to A Street. The adjoining triangular plot extending to the north, from A Street to Maryland Avenue, he numbered

727.[2] This land was soon to be appraised at six cents per front foot.

By 1793, with elaborate Masonic ceremony, the cornerstone of the northern section of the Capitol Building was laid on Capitol Hill. The Capitol resembled but little the structure we know today. It had no dome. It had neither of its present wings. It consisted of the two rectangular structures that today constitute the elements immediately north and south of the dome. Congress and the Supreme Court met in those buildings. There Jefferson and Madison were each twice inaugurated as President.

Residences sprang up in the neighborhood. Then, during Madison's second term, came the War of 1812. On August 24, 1814, the British invaded Washington. Marching from Bladensburg down what is now Maryland Avenue, they met little opposition. It is said, however, that, as they reached Second Street, at least one shot was fired at them. It killed the British General's horse and, in retaliation, the house from which the shot had come was burned by the invaders. They also seriously damaged with fire both of the buildings that constituted the Capitol.

3. 1815-1819 Produced the Brick Capitol

The British withdrew as suddenly as they had come. The Government of the United States returned to Washington. The President and Mrs. Madison moved into the Octagon House at 18th Street and New York Avenue, N. W. The Thirteenth Congress convened on September 19, 1814, in special session, at Blodgett's "Great Hotel" at Seventh and Eighth Streets between E and F Streets, N. W. On September 21 the House of Representatives defeated, 54 to 83, a proposal to remove the seat of Government from the District. Somewhat later the Senate took similar action. The immediate need being for a temporary Capitol Building, fate led the way to the vacant southeast corner of First and A

Streets, N. E., where there bloomed a flower garden. To the east of it was Walker's (or Tunnicliffe's) Hotel. Anxious to retain the seat of Government in Washington, a group of citizens promptly raised, by private subscription, $25,000. This proved to be enough to buy this corner and to build there a temporary Capitol.[3]

July 4, 1815, its cornerstone was laid. The structure rose to three stories. The Senate Chamber was on the ground floor. The Hall of the House of Representatives was on the floor above. Congress approved the building and occupied it, paying for its use $1,650 a year which represented 6 percent on the investment, plus $150 for insurance. Congress paid $5,000 more for furnishings, including the later famous red leather chairs for the Senators. On December 4, 1815, the Fourteenth Congress met briefly at Blodgett's Hotel but by December 13 both Houses of Congress were in the new "Brick Capitol." Vice President Elbridge Gerry of Massachusetts having passed away, the presiding officer of the Senate was its President pro tempore, Senator John Gaillard of South Carolina. The Speaker of the House was Henry Clay of Kentucky. The Fifteenth Congress, throughout its life, also met in the Brick Capitol, adjourning *sine die* March 3, 1819. The presiding officer of the Senate for that session was Vice President Daniel D. Tompkins of New York. The Speaker of the House again was Henry Clay of Kentucky.[4]

In December, 1819, the Sixteenth Congress convened in the newly rebuilt and permanent Capitol Building on the crest of "The Hill." Its reconstruction had been made possible by a $500,000 loan to the Government from the Washington banks. The Supreme Court preceded Congress in its return to the permanent Capitol. There the Court met in the semicircular room on the ground floor under the Senate Chamber.

The most unusual incident that had occurred in the Brick Capitol, while Congress occupied it, was connected with the inauguration of President Monroe and Vice President Tompkins on March 4, 1817. The advance arrangements for the ceremony conformed largely to previous custom, except that, instead of holding the ceremony in the small Senate Chamber, the plan was to move the red leather Senate chairs into the Hall of the House of Representatives. However, the Speaker of the House had not been consulted and, when confronted with the plan, Henry Clay objected, particularly to the presence of the Senate chairs in the House of Representatives. The arrangements were quickly changed. Vice President Tompkins was inducted into office in the Senate Chamber and there made his response, but President-elect Monroe was taken out-of-doors to a temporary portico which had been erected on First Street, directly in front of the building. There in the presence of the general public, the oath of office was administered to him by Chief Justice Marshall. There the President delivered his inaugural address and thus set the precedent for public inaugurals.[5]

4. 1819-1824 Brought the Circuit Court for the District of Columbia

When Congress returned to the permanent Capitol, it crowded out the Circuit Court for the District of Columbia. That court, in turn, was allotted space vacated in the Brick Capitol. There it met from 1819 to 1824. Pressure from the local bar induced it to move downtown to Judiciary Square where it occupied space in the new City Hall at the head of what is now John Marshall Place.

5. From About 1824 to 1861 the Site Was Used for a Lodging House, Including an Occupancy by John C. Calhoun—1849-1850

Some time after the Old Brick Capitol ceased to be used by the Circuit Court, it was converted into a lodging house.

[69]

In 1841 we find H. V. Hill advertising furnished rooms for rent. Several members of Congress lived there.[6] It housed two clubs for young men. Its most prominent tenant was Senator John C. Calhoun from South Carolina. Formerly Secretary of War, Secretary of State, and twice Vice President, he was completing forty years of public service. There Senator Calhoun lived, largely alone, from 1849 until his death at the age of sixty-eight, on Sunday, March 31, 1850. It was there that his political opponent, but personal friend, Senator Daniel Webster of Massachusetts, came to cheer him during his final days.

6. *From 1861 to 1868 the Site Was Occupied by the Capitol Prison*

After an interval, during part of which the building was used as a public school, the site at First and A Streets, N. E., passed into the sixth period of its career. In the spring of 1861, the Old Brick Capitol was converted into a Federal Military Prison. It was known as the Capitol Prison. A high wall was built around the prison yard on the east. The prison was used for "state prisoners" rather than for violators of military discipline. During its first four months only fifteen prisoners were sent there. Soon, however, arrests became so numerous that two houses in the adjoining block to the south were used to house the overflow. At one time, 1004 prisoners are said to have been crowded in. Among its notorious inmates were the Confederate spies, Rose Greenhow and Belle Boyd. Captain Henry Wirz, former Commandant of the Andersonville Confederate Military Prison, was another. He was hanged in the prison yard on November 10, 1865, and at least three others are said to have been executed there.

7. From About 1867 to 1921 the Site Again Became Residential. It Included the Residence of Justice Field from 1869 to 1899

In May, 1867, the Old Brick Capitol property and its grounds were sold for $20,000 to George T. Brown, Sergeant-at-Arms of the Senate. With financial aid from Senator Lyman Trumbull of Illinois, he remodeled and converted the building into three large row houses. They were four stories high and faced First Street on the southeast corner of the A Street intersection. Known as Trumbull Row, numbers 21, 23 and 25, they provided convenient and desirable living quarters.

The most famous occupant of these houses was Justice Stephen J. Field of the Supreme Court of the United States. Appointed to that Court in 1863, he spent much time on the Pacific Coast in performance of his duties as a Circuit Justice. However, in 1870 or 1871, he established his residence in Trumbull Row. He occupied the house at the southerly end of the row which had been acquired by one or more of his brothers, Cyrus, David Dudley and Henry.[7] He built an addition to it and provided a large reception room on the first floor. His library of 3000 volumes was on the second floor. There he followed a tireless schedule that began at seven o'clock each morning. At the age of eighty-two he died there on Sunday, April 9, 1899. This was nearly two years after he had submitted his resignation from the Court to take effect December 1, 1897, closing the longest term of office ever served on that Court—thirty-four years, eight months and twenty days.[8]

8. From 1921 to 1928 the Site Was the Headquarters of the National Woman's Party

Mrs. Alva Belmont (Mrs. Oliver Hazard Perry Belmont), having acquired the Old Brick Capitol property, presented it to the National Woman's Party as a permanent headquarters for their crusade for equal rights for women. Known as No. 21 First Street, N. E., it was cherished by that organization not only as a headquarters but also as an historical shrine. They embellished the grounds with a garden. When, in 1928, this site was selected for the Supreme Court Building, the National Woman's Party opposed the selection because it meant the removal of their historic building. The Senate adopted a resolution favoring the retention of their building and the abandonment of the proposal to build the Supreme Court Building there. However, Case No. 1911 in the Supreme Court of the District of Columbia resulted in the condemnation of the property and an award to the National Woman's Party of substantially $300,000 as just compensation for the taking of it.[9] The Party thereupon moved to its present headquarters in the historic mansion on the northwest corner of Constitution Avenue (old B Street) and Second Street, N. E.

9. *Since 1928 the Site Has Been Set Aside for the Supreme Court of the United States*

Completed in 1935 the Supreme Court Building, designed by Cass Gilbert, Sr., Cass Gilbert, Jr., and John R. Rockart, stands where First and A Streets formerly met. The site is now known as Number One First Street, N. E. The Supreme Court Building provides a fitting climax. Magnificent in design, its central element reflects the proportions of the Parthenon of Athens. Significant as a symbol of the independence of the judiciary, it honors an historic spot. Inspirational in its message of "Equal Justice Under Law," it expresses in fitting form the Faith of our Fathers.

NOTES TO CHAPTER IV

1. Within that area, the Duddington mansion house was completed in about 1797. For more than a century it was to stand between First and

Second Streets, S. E., near E Street. The neighborhood became known as Carroll Springs. Its location is roughly indicated now by that of Carroll Street, which extends one block, from First to Second Street, S. E., between Streets C and D. The house at the southeast corner of First and C Streets is still marked Duddington Place. A later development was that of the Carroll Row Houses, on the site of the Congressional Library. Their presence is not now commemorated unless it be in the name of the Carroll Arms Hotel on First Street, N. E., several blocks to the north. At the south end of the Carroll property and reaching to the Anacostia River, there was developed a sparsely settled area called Carrollsburg. Its name survives at Carrollsburg Place, which extends from M Street to N Street, S. W., in the block just west of South Capitol Street.

2. "A" Street then opened directly into First Street. Its north side followed the line now marked by the north wall of the north wing of the Supreme Court Building. Its south side followed a line which now would pass through that wing between its fourth and fifth windows from the north.

3. The largest subscriber was Daniel Carroll of Duddington. The next largest was Thomas Law. Like Carroll, he was a substantial property owner. He also was a brother of Lord Ellenborough, Lord Chief Justice of the King's Bench of England. I Bryan, A History of the National Capital (1914); Busey, Pictures of the City of Washington in the Past (1898), 129.

4. In the Brick Capitol during these two Congresses were heard many leaders of their day. Among these were Senator Rufus King, of New York, later an unsuccessful candidate for President of the United States; Representative Philip P. Barbour, of Virginia, later a Justice of the Supreme Court; John C. Calhoun, of South Carolina, later Vice President of the United States; William Henry Harrison, of Ohio, later President of the United States; John McLean, of Ohio, later a Justice of the Supreme Court; John Randolph, of Virginia, later a Senator from that State; John Tyler, of Virginia, later President of the United States; and Daniel Webster, then representing New Hampshire but later to become Secretary of State and a Senator from Massachusetts.

5. An echo of this was heard in the Senate twenty years later, preceding the inauguration of President Van Buren. Clay was then a Senator and inquired why it was that the Senate, rather than the House of Representatives, had "the exclusive care" of administering the Presidential oath. He recalled the incident at the Old Brick Capitol, in 1817, and furnished what is probably our most authentic account of it. His colloquy of February 28, 1837, is reported in Vol. 13, Pt. 1, of Gales and Seaton's Register of Debates in Congress, 24th Cong., 2d Sess. at 992, as follows:

"THE PRESIDENT pro tem presented a letter from the President elect of the United States, informing the Senate that he would be ready to take the usual oath of office on Saturday, March 4, at 12 o'clock, noon, at such place and in such manner as the Senate might designate.

"MR. GRUNDY [of Tennessee] offered a resolution for the appointment of a committee of arrangements, to make the requisite preparations for administering the oath to the President elect of the United States.

"MR. CLAY [of Kentucky] said he would like to inquire whether precedents had been examined on this subject. He was aware that the Senate had always had a peculiar agency in this business; but he was not aware why the Senate should act upon it any more than the House, or why it was not a joint concern. He remembered that, on the first election of Mr. Monroe, the committee of the Senate applied to him, as Speaker of the House, for the use of the chamber of the House; and he had told them that he would put the chamber in order for the use of the Senate, but the control of it he did not feel authorized to surrender. They wished also to bring in the fine red chairs of the Senate, but he told them it could not be done; the plain democratic chairs of the House were more becoming. The consequence was, that Mr. Monroe, instead of taking the oath within doors, took it outside, in the open air, in front of the Capitol. Mr. C. mentioned this for the purpose of making the inquiry, what was the practice, and on what it was founded, and why the Senate had the exclusive care of administering the oath.

"MR. GRUNDY said the committee had found no authority but several precedents, which were in strict accordance with the proposition now proposed to be made. He did not recollect any instance in which the House had participated in it; and, in fact, the House, as such, had no existence, their term having expired on the preceding day. The committee had examined three cases of more modern date, and had found nothing in opposition to the practice proposed. If the committee could not get into the House, they could go out of doors.

"The resolution was adopted, and the Chair was authorized to appoint the above-named committee of three members."

6. Representatives William H. Brockenborough of Florida, Reuben Chapman of Alabama, Joseph A. Woodward of South Carolina, and Isaac E. Morse of Louisiana are among those reported to have lived there in the 1840's.

7. Cyrus W. Field was the projector of the first Atlantic Cable. David Dudley Field was the author of the Code of Civil Procedure adopted by New York and followed by many western states. For many years the four brothers met annually with Justice Field at this house to celebrate the birthday of David Dudley Field on February 13.

8. There also once stood in this block an historic home on East Capitol Street occupied by Captain William Easby, a veteran of the Battle of Bladensburg in 1814. It was built in 1750 by Daniel Carroll and came into the ownership of the Easby family in about 1824.

9. The parcel acquired from the National Woman's Party was the largest one in the site. The condemnation awards for the entire site came to $1,768,141.

PRINCIPAL REFERENCES

Brown, George Rothwell, Washington—A Not Too Serious History (1930).

Bryan, W. B., A History of the National Capital, Vols. I and II (1914).

Busey, Samuel C., Pictures of the City of Washington in the Past (1898).

Coit, Margaret L., John C. Calhoun (1950).

Equal Rights, Vol. XIV, pp. 153, 157, 163, 231, 371 (1928).

Final Report of the United States Supreme Court Building Commission, S. Doc. No. 88 (76th Cong., 1st Sess. (1939)).

Hazelton, George C., Jr., The National Capital—Its Architecture, Art and History (1902).

Proctor, John Clagett, Proctor's Washington (1949).

Semmes, Raphael, Captains and Mariners of Early Maryland (1937).

Swisher, Carl B., Stephen J. Field, Craftsman of the Law (1930).

————————◆————————

In Civil War days, John Hitz, the first Swiss Consul-General to the United States, and great-grandfather of Justice Harold Hitz Burton, maintained his home and his consulate at 29 A Street, S. E., within what is now the Capitol Plaza, opposite the Congressional Library. At his death in 1864 President Lincoln and Secretary of State Seward attended his funeral services at that residence.

V

The Dartmouth College Case

A DRAMATIZATION*

THE LEGAL SIGNIFICANCE of the Dartmouth College case[1] has been amply analyzed elsewhere. This statement presents its dramatic quality. Although staged as a three-act play its essential action is authentic. The principal characters are John Wheelock, onetime president of Dartmouth College and Dartmouth University, Daniel Webster, of counsel for the trustees of the college, and John Marshall, Chief Justice of the Supreme Court of the United States. The action takes place in New Hampshire and Washington, D. C., between 1800 and 1820.

PROLOGUE

In 1800, in the office of President Wheelock of Dartmouth College, at Hanover, N. H. President Wheelock is talking with Daniel Webster, an 18-year-old student.

Daniel voices his appreciation of the intellectual world the college has opened to him. He explains how his pioneering father, Captain Ebenezer Webster, had sacrificed the family's interests to send him to Dartmouth and how Daniel plans to help his brother follow him.

Dr. Wheelock tells how his father, Reverend Eleazar Wheelock, about forty-five years ago, had established, at his own expense, and on his own estate, a charity school for the instructions of Indians in the Christian religion. To this end he secured funds from the Earl of Dartmouth and other English sponsors. To perpetuate his program, he sought a corporate charter for a college. Its trustees were to develop the Indian Charity School independently of the college, and

* Reprinted by permission of the American Bar Association Journal.

Dartmouth College itself was to provide higher education for English and other youths, as well as Indians.

On December 13, 1769, Governor John Wentworth of the Province of New Hampshire, in the name of George III, granted the charter. It ran to The Trustees of Dartmouth College. It prescribed a quorum of seven, "the whole number of said trustees consisting, and hereafter forever to consist, of twelve, and no more...."[2]

It named the original twelve and authorized the trustees thereafter to fill vacancies in their body. The trustees were to hold title to the college properties, appoint its president, professors, officers and other representatives, grant its degrees and govern its affairs. The charter named Eleazar Wheelock as the "founder" of the college, appointed him its first president and authorized him, by his last will, to name his successor to serve unless and until disapproved by the trustees.

The college was established on the Connecticut River at Hanover. New Hampshire lands were granted to it by that State and Vermont lands by the Governor of Vermont. President Eleazar Wheelock died in 1779. By his will he had named as his successor his son, Lieutenant Colonel John Wheelock, who at once gave up his Army career to devote himself to the college.

In 1800 the students number nearly 150 and Dartmouth is the only institution of higher education in New Hampshire. Daniel catches the spirit of the dauntless founder of this college in the forest, dedicated to the intellectual and spiritual advancement of mankind forever. He expresses the hope that some day he may repay a part of his personal debt to Dartmouth.

Act I. *The Issue is Created*

Scene 1

The Trustees Act

August 26, 1815, in a meeting of the trustees of
Dartmouth College, at Hanover, N. H.

President John Wheelock refers to the steady increase of
his disagreements with the trustees since 1809. Led by United
States Senator Thomas W. Thompson,[3] they in turn charge
him with starting a bitter war of pamphlets by making false
charges against them and attacking their authority to guide
the corporate policy of the college. They protest his having
memorialized the Legislature to investigate the trustees' conduct of the college. He replies that he has gone further and
already has appeared before the Legislative Committee.[4]
Some trustees urge patience but the majority cannot be restrained. Accusing Wheelock of disrupting the college, they
remove him from office as president and trustee. Two protest.[5]

Scene 2

The Legislature Acts

June 26, 1816, in a cloakroom of the New Hampshire House of
Representatives at Concord, N. H. The business before the
House is a bill "to amend the charter, and enlarge and improve
the Corporation of Dartmouth College."

The conversation discloses that in March, 1816, the Anti-
Federalists had elected William Plumer as Governor. June 6,
in his message to the Legislature, he had urged that the college charter be amended, especially so as to terminate the
authority of the trustees to name their successors and so as to
require its president to report annually to the Governor upon
the state of the college.[6]
The bill before the House includes amendments to the
college charter (1) changing its name to Dartmouth University; (2) increasing its trustees from twelve to twenty-

one and its quorum from seven to eleven; (3) adding a Board of Overseers of twenty-five members, with a quorum of fifteen; (4) authorizing all original and subsequent vacancies among trustees and overseers to be filled with appointees of the Governor and Council, except that the President of the Senate and the Speaker of the House of Representatives of New Hampshire, and the Governor and Lieutenant Governor of Vermont, shall be overseers ex-officio; (5) the president and professors of the college shall be nominated by the trustees and approved by the overseers; (6) the overseers may disapprove any action of the trustees provided they do so within sixty days after receipt of copies of the action; and (7) the president shall render an annual report to the Governor.[7]

The bill is ably debated. Written remonstrances from United States Senator and College Trustee Thomas W. Thompson and others are before the body.[8] The point is clearly made that this college was founded and endowed by private individuals, rather than by the King or the Government and that, if this property has been misapplied by its trustees, it is for the judiciary and not for the Legislature to determine that issue. Nevertheless, the bill passes by a small majority.[9]

SCENE 3

The College Carries On

February 28, 1817, in Rowley Hall, Hanover, N. H., President Brown
of the college is meeting with Professors Ebenezer Adams
and Roswell Shurtleff

Brown reports that under the reduced quorum amendment of December 18, the university trustees voted to remove him as president and to reinstate John Wheelock, with William Allen as acting president due to Wheelock's ill health.[10] Brown further reports that the university boards have elected, as secretary and treasurer, William H. Woodward, who had been the college secretary; have placed the corporate records and seal of the college in Woodward's possession; have removed four trustees and all members of the faculty who adhered to the old board; and have ousted the officers and faculty from the college buildings. The ousted trustees, officers, faculty and their students have moved to nearby Rowley Hall. There they carry on their educational program. Scarcely any students attend the newly constituted and competing university.

The college has sought the legal advice of Senator Jeremiah Mason,[11] Judge Jeremiah Smith[12] and Representative Daniel Webster.[13] Each has high standing at the Bar and in public life. February 8, 1817, at their suggestion, a test case already has been filed in the Common Pleas Court of Grafton County, New Hampshire, against William H. Woodward attacking his right to the possession of the college records, seal and other corporate property. Upon an agreed statement of facts the case is pending in the Superior Court of Judicature of New Hampshire, which is the state's highest tribunal.[14]

Brown, Adams and Shurtleff sign "An Address of the Executive Officers of Dartmouth College to the Publick." It states their case. Believing in the righteousness of their cause and its importance to the college and to others in like situations, they firmly resolve to accept the risk of prosecution and to "continue to instruct the classes committed to them . . . until the decision of the law shall convince them of their error, or restore them to their rights."[15]

Act II. *The State Court Decides*

November 6, 1817. In the Courtroom of the Superior Court of Judicature of New Hampshire, at Plymouth, Grafton County, N. H. On the bench: Chief Justice William M. Richardson,[16] Justice Samuel Bell[17] and Justice Levi Woodbury.[18] Among those at the bar are former Senator Mason, Judge Smith and former Representative Webster as counsel for the trustees.[19] Attorney General George Sullivan[20] and Ichabod Bartlett[21] are present as counsel for the opposition.

The Chief Justice announces the unanimous opinion of the court in *The Trustees of Dartmouth College* v. *Woodward*.[22]

The court faces squarely the contention of the trustees that the Amendatory Acts exceed the legislative powers of the Legislature and violate the Constitutions of New Hampshire and the United States. It sustains the legislation at every point. It holds the corporation to be a public corporation subject to this kind of control in the public interest. In view of the proceedings to come, the following quotations are especially significant:

The office of trustee of Dartmouth College is, in fact, a publick trust, as much so as the office of governor, or of judge of this court; . . . .

It becomes then unnecessary to decide in this case, how far the legislature possesses a constitutional right to interfere in the concerns of *private corporations*. . . .

These [amendatory] acts compel the old trustees to sacrifice no private interest whatever, but merely to admit others to aid them, in the management of the concerns of a publick institution: . . . .

If the charter of a publick institution, like that of Dartmouth College, is to be construed as a contract, within the intent of the constitution of the United States, it will, in our opinion, be difficult to say what powers, in relation to their publick institutions, if any, are left to the states. It is a construction, in our view, repugnant to the very principles of all government, because it places all the publick institutions of all the states beyond legislative controul. . . .

We are therefore clearly of opinion, that the charter of Dartmouth College is not a contract, within the meaning of this clause in the constitution of the United States.[23]

ACT III. *In the Supreme Court of the United States*

SCENE I

Webster's Argument

March 10, 1818, 11 A.M. In the temporary courtroom of the Supreme Court of the United States—a plain committee room in the partially restored Capitol, in Washington, D. C. Webster and Joseph Hopkinson are ready to proceed for the trustees in the Dartmouth College case.[24] Representative John Holmes[25] and Attorney General William Wirt[26] oppose them.

The Court is announced by the crier.[27] All its members are present—Chief Justice Marshall and Justice Washington, both from Virginia and appointees of President Adams, Justices William Johnson of South Carolina, Livingston of New York and Todd of Kentucky, appointees of President Jefferson, and Justices Duvall of Maryland and Story of Massachusetts, appointees of President Madison.

There are no printed or written briefs in the hands of the Court. The case is called and Webster rises. It is his first major case before the Supreme Court. Justice Story takes up his pen to make his customary full notes but becomes so absorbed in the argument that his pen remains poised and he takes no notes.[28]

Although stating that the sole issue before this Court is the violation of Article I, §10, of the Federal Constitution,[29] Webster builds a background for the meaning of its language. In doing so, he summarizes the arguments made by Mason and Smith in the state court knowing also that those arguments may later come squarely before this Court through new test cases. He argues that the charter amendments are beyond the proper scope of legislative power. He cites *Fletcher* v. *Peck*[30] to show that a state contract contains obligations protected by the Contract Clause and *New Jersey*

v. *Wilson*[31] to the effect that the obligations of a contract made by the King before the Revolution are as much entitled to protection as those made by a state thereafter. He demonstrates that The Trustees of Dartmouth College constitute a private eleemosynary corporation rather than a public corporation and argues that a state legislature which cannot repeal its grant of such a private corporate charter likewise cannot impair or essentially alter that charter without the assent of the corporation.[32]

At that point, tradition has it, Webster completed his three-hour legal argument and addressed a famous emotional peroration to the Chief Justice. The best authenticated version of it is as follows:

> "*This, sir, is my case!* It is the case, not merely of that humble institution, it is the case of every college in our land. It is more. It is the case of every eleemosynary institution throughout our country—of all those great charities founded by the piety of our ancestors to alleviate human misery, and scatter blessings along the pathway of life. It is more! It is, in some sense, the case of every man among us who has property of which he may be stripped; for the question is simply this: Shall our State Legislatures be allowed to take that which is not their own, to turn it from its original use, and apply it to such ends or purposes as they, in their discretion, shall see fit!
>
> "Sir, you may destroy this little institution; it is weak; it is in your hands! I know it is one of the lesser lights in the literary horizon of our country. You may put it out. But if you do so, you must carry through your work! You must extinguish, one after another, all those great lights of science, which, for more than a century, have thrown their radiance over our land!
>
> "It is, sir, as I have said, a small college. And yet *there are those who love it*—"

Here the feelings which he had thus far succeeded in keeping down broke forth. His lips quivered; his firm cheeks trembled with emotion; his eyes were filled with tears, his voice choked, and he seemed struggling to the utmost simply to gain that mastery over himself which might save him from an unmanly burst of feeling. . . . [In a] few broken words of tenderness . . . he went on to speak of his attachment to the college. The whole seemed to be mingled throughout with the recollections of father, mother, brother, and all the trials and privations through which he had made his way into life. Every one saw that it was wholly unpremeditated, a pressure on his heart, which sought relief in words and tears.

The court-room during these two or three minutes presented an extraordinary spectacle. Chief Justice Marshall, with his tall and gaunt figure bent over as if to catch the slightest whisper, the deep furrows of his cheek expanded with emotion, and eyes suffused with tears; Mr. Justice Washington at his side—with his small and emaciated frame, and countenance . . . like marble . . . leaning forward with an eager, troubled look; and the remainder of the court, at the two extremities, pressing, as it were, toward a single point, while the audience below were wrapping themselves round in closer folds beneath the bench to catch each look, and every movement of the speaker's face. If a painter could give us the scene on canvas—those forms and countenances, and Daniel Webster as he then stood in the midst, it would be one of the most touching pictures in the history of eloquence. . . . the *pathetic* depends not merely on the words uttered, but still more on the estimate we put upon him who utters them. There was not one among the strong-minded men of that assembly who could think it unmanly to weep, when he saw standing before him the man who had made such an argument, melted into the tenderness of a child.

Mr. Webster had now recovered his composure, and fixing his keen eye on the Chief Justice, said, in that deep tone with which he sometimes thrilled the hearts of an audience—

"Sir, I know not how others may feel" (glancing at the

opponents of the college before him), "but, for myself, when I see my Alma Mater surrounded, like Caesar in the senate-house, by those who are reiterating stab upon stab, I would not, for this right hand, have her turn to me, and say, *Et tu quoque, mi filii! And thou too, my son!*"

He sat down. There was a deathlike stillness throughout the room for some moments; every one seemed to be slowly recovering himself, and coming gradually back to his ordinary range of thought and feeling.[33]

Scene 2

Pending the Decision

September, 1818, in Rowley Hall, Hanover, N. H., President Brown and Daniel Webster are in consultation.

President Brown asks Webster about the argument in Washington. Webster sketches the course of the three-day hearing. In his own opening he had combined Mason's and Smith's arguments in the state court with his and had concluded with a "Caesar in the Senate-House" peroration somewhat as he had done at Exeter in 1817.

The university trustees had thought it a needless expense to send to Washington Sullivan and Bartlett, who had so ably represented them in New Hampshire. In their stead, Representative Holmes, of the District of Maine, had spoken three hours in reply to Webster. His presentation was more of a stump speech than a legal argument. In the midst of it, Justice Bell of New Hampshire, who was in the audience, seized his hat and dashed out of the courtroom. The newly installed Attorney General Wirt closed for the university. Although an eloquent speaker and a competent lawyer, he had argued six cases in the Supreme Court between February 2 and March 11, and had not had the time needed to study this case. For example, he had built part of his argument on the theory that the King, rather than Eleazar Wheelock who had originated the school, taught in it, and raised the funds for it, was its founder. When it was pointed out to him that the charter itself named Wheelock as the founder, Wirt shifted his ground and asked that he be allowed to resume his argument the next day. Wirt also had inserted an emotional touch in his peroration when he sought to turn back on Webster the latter's reference to Caesar. Evidently referring to the late President Wheelock's disappointment when Webster had failed to appear with him before a Legislative Committee in 1816, Wirt summoned up the ghost of John Wheelock to point his finger at Webster and to quote, in closing, Caesar's famous ejaculation "*Et tu, Brute?*"[34]

In contrast to the inadequacy of the arguments for the university, Joseph Hopkinson closed for the college trustees with an admirable summary showing an understanding of every part of the case.

The next day, the Chief Justice announced that the Justices had conferred on the case, that some had not come to an opinion on it, that those who had opinions did not agree and the cause must therefore be continued until the next term.[35]

Webster had written to Judge Smith that "The chief and Washington, I have no doubt, are with us. Duvall and Todd perhaps against us; the other three holding up. I cannot much doubt but that Story will be with us in the end, and I think we have much more than an even chance for one of the others."[36]

Webster recognizes that the New Hampshire Court's opinion is "able, ingenious, and plausible" and is receiving wide circulation in printed form. To offset this, he has sent to Justice Story five copies of a privately printed edition of his own argument.[37]

Brown advises Webster that Chancellor James Kent of the New York Court of Chancery has read the New Hampshire decision and has indicated an inclination to agree with it. He fears that Kent's view may reach Justices Livingston or

Johnson, who occasionally confer with the Chancellor on legal questions of the day. To offset this, Webster agrees that Brown should visit the Chancellor at Albany and leave with him the college's printed arguments.

Webster reports also that three new test suits have been filed on behalf of the college. These are actions in ejectment filed in the Federal Circuit Court because of diversity of citizenship, all with the purpose of broadening the scope of review by the Supreme Court of the United States in the event that the college loses on the constitutional issue now under advisement.

Finally they discuss the report that the university is retaining William Pinkney, a leader of the Maryland Bar,[38] to seek a rehearing of the case in the Supreme Court.

Scene 3

The Final Decision

February 2, 1819, 10:55 A.M. In the newly decorated Supreme Court Chamber in the Capitol at Washington. It is the second day of the term. Many lawyers and spectators, including Webster, Hopkinson and Pinkney, are assembled.

Webster and Hopkinson express to each other the hope that the Dartmouth College decision will come down. Pinkney stands close to the bench with a view to catching the eye of the Chief Justice in order to move for a rehearing in the college case. At 11 the Court is announced and enters. All members are present except Justice Todd. Mr. Pinkney steps forward to address the Court. The Chief Justice looks the other way and announces that the Court has reached a decision in Case No. 25, The Trustees of Dartmouth College *v.* William Woodward. His opinion covers about thirty pages. He cites no cases but demonstrates his propositions with characteristic clearness. Obviously the decision is a landmark. Among its principal points are the following:

. . . On the judges of this Court . . . is imposed the high

and solemn duty of protecting, from even legislative violation, those contracts which the constitution of our country
has placed beyond legislative control; and, however irk-
some the task may be, this is a duty from which we dare
not shrink.

It becomes then the duty of the Court most seriously to
examine this charter, and to ascertain its true character.

From this review of the charter, it appears, that Dartmouth College is an eleemosynary institution, incorporated for the purpose of perpetuating the application of
the bounty of the donors, to the specified objects of that
bounty; that its trustees or governors were originally
named by the founder, and invested with the power of
perpetuating themselves; that they are not public officers,
nor is it a civil institution, participating in the administration of government; but a charity school, or a seminary of
education, incorporated for the preservation of its property, and the perpetual application of that property to the
objects of its creation.

This is plainly a contract to which the donors, the trustees, and the crown, (to whose rights and obligations
New-Hampshire succeeds) were the original parties. It is
a contract made on a valuable consideration. It is a contract for the security and disposition of property. It is a
contract, on the faith of which, real and personal estate
has been conveyed to the corporation. It is then a contract
within the letter of the constitution, and within its spirit
also, unless the fact, that the property is invested by the
donors in trustees for the promotion of religion and education, for the benefit of persons who are perpetually
changing, though the objects remain the same, shall create
a particular exception, taking this case out of the prohibi-
tion contained in this constitution.

. . . It is not enough to say, that this particular case was
not in the mind of the Convention, when the article was
framed, nor of the American people, when it was adopted.
It is necessary to go farther, and to say that, had this par-

ticular case been suggested, the language would have been so varied, as to exclude it, or it would have been made a special exception. . . .

The opinion of the Court, after mature deliberation, is, that this is a contract, the obligation of which cannot be impaired, without violating the constitution of the United States. . . .

. . . We next proceed to the inquiry, whether its obligation has been impaired by those acts of the legislature of New-Hampshire, to which the special verdict refers.

By the revolution, the duties, as well as the powers, of government devolved on the people of New-Hampshire. It is admitted, that among the latter was comprehended the transcendent power of parliament, as well as that of the executive department. . . . But the constitution of the United States has imposed this additional limitation, that the legislature of a State shall pass no act "impairing the obligation of contracts."

. . . The whole power of governing the college is transferred [by the amendments] from trustees appointed according to the will of the founder, expressed in the charter, to the executive of New-Hampshire. . . . The will of the State is substituted for the will of the donors, in every essential operation of the college. This is not an immaterial change. . . . The charter of 1769 exists no longer. It is reorganized; and reorganized in such a manner, as to convert a literary institution, moulded according to the will of its founders, and placed under the control of private literary men, into a machine entirely subservient to the will of government. This may be for the advantage of this college in particular, and may be for the advantage of literature in general; but it is not according to the will of the donors, and is subversive of that contract, on the faith of which their property was given.

It results from this opinion, that the acts of the legislature of New-Hampshire . . . are repugnant to the constitution of the United States; and that the judgment of this special verdict ought to have been for the plaintiffs. The judgment of the State Court must, therefore, be reversed.[39]

No other opinions are read.[40] Justice Duvall notes his dissent. No mention is made of Justice Todd. The case is closed. The Dartmouth College charter of 1769 is a contract forever binding upon both the trustees and the State.[41]

NOTES TO CHAPTER V

1. *The Trustees of Dartmouth College* v. *Woodward*, 4 Wheat. 518.

2. 4 Wheat. 525.
The trustees were given wide authority to make rules—
"not repugnant to the laws and statutes of our realm of Great Britain, or of this our province of New-Hampshire, and not excluding any person of any religious denomination whatsoever, from free and equal liberty and advantage of education, or from any of the liberties and privileges or immunities of the said college, on account of his or their speculative sentiments in religion, and of his or their being of a religious profession different from the said trustees. . . ." *Id.*, at 533.

3. A trustee from 1802 to 1817, graduate of Harvard, gentleman and lawyer of the old school, rich and courtly, a patron of Daniel Webster, and United States Senator from New Hampshire 1814-1817. Shirley, The Dartmouth College Causes and the Supreme Court (1879) 81, 83-84; Biographical Directory of the American Congress (1950) 1915.

4. A misunderstanding between Wheelock and Webster arose in this connection. In the spring of 1815, Wheelock, contemplating personal litigation against the college for money due him and on other grounds, had suggested to Webster that he might wish to retain his professional services. Webster had indicated his willingness to serve him. On August 5, when Wheelock learned that legislative hearings as to the college would begin August 16, he wrote to Webster urgently requesting the latter's appearance with him at the hearings. Webster received the letter too late to attend the hearings and Wheelock had to proceed alone. Webster also explained, later, that court engagements would have prevented his attendance in any event, and that he had not regarded this request as a professional call. Furthermore, he was not convinced that Wheelock was wholly right on the issues before the committee and he had no inclination to espouse either side of the college controversy, except in proceedings in which his services were "professional." Shirley, 86-92; Farrar, Dartmouth College Case (1819), 379-380, 390-391.

5. Those protesting were Governor Gilman of New Hampshire and Judge Stephen Jacob of Vermont. Two days later the trustees elected Reverend Francis Brown, of Maine, president of the college. Accepting the office at 31, he served with "rare tact and administrative genius," but died

July 27, 1820, after steering the college successfully through its greatest crisis. Shirley, 100-101. Most of New Hampshire and much of New England had taken sides. Orthodox Congregationalists and Federalists generally had supported the trustees. The other denominations and Anti-Federalists generally had supported Wheelock.

6. Shirley, 106.

7. See 4 Wheat. 539-544; Farrar, 18-22, for the Act in full.

8. His remonstrances of June 19 and 24, 1816, charge that the Legislature is about to take action without considering the report of the Legislature's own Fact Finding Committee. He warns that the "tendency of this bill . . . is to convert the peaceful retreat of our college into a field for party warfare." See Farrar, 385-391; Smith, Dartmouth College (1878), 101-106.

9. In the Senate a proposal to make the amendment subject to approval by the trustees was defeated. The bill was approved by the Governor June 27, 1816. Seventy-five of the 190 members of the House recorded their protest in the journal, declaring that the charter was a contract and that the trustees could not lawfully be deprived of their rights under it in the face of the federal constitutional provision against the impairment of the obligation of contracts. Shirley, 109-110; Farrar, 381, 389-390.

The Governor and the Council at once named appointees to fill all of the newly created positions. Meetings of the university boards were called for August 26, 1816. Only ten of the trustees and fourteen of the overseers were present. The attendance thus fell one member short of a quorum on each board. On August 28, nine of the twelve previously constituted college trustees declared that the amendment was unlawful and that they felt obliged to refuse to act under it. Farrar, 379-384.

On December 18, 1816, the Legislature passed a supplementary Act permitting adjournments by less than a quorum of each board, reducing the trustees' quorum to nine, with the concurrence of six trustees necessary to take action. A third Act, approved December 26, prescribed a $500 penalty for hindering officers acting under the amendments. 4 Wheat. 545-549; Farrar, 23-26.

10. Wheelock died April 11, 1817, leaving $40,000 by will to the university.

11. An impressive figure, 6 feet 7 inches tall, he was as large in mind as he was in body. A Federalist, he had served as Attorney General of the State 1802-1805, as United States Senator 1813-1817 when he resigned. He had declined appointment by Governor Plumer as Chief Justice of the Superior Court of New Hampshire in August, 1816.

12. A Federalist, he served in Congress 1791-1797, as United States District Attorney 1797-1800; Judge of Probate 1800-1802; United States Circuit Judge 1801-1802; Chief Justice of the Superior Court of New Hampshire 1802-1809; Governor 1809-1810; and Chief Justice of the then styled Supreme Court of New Hampshire 1813-1816.

13. Webster was thirty-five and on the threshold of his professional and political career. A Federalist, he had served in Congress as a Representative from New Hampshire March 4, 1813-March 3, 1817. He then moved

to Boston and was in active practice there throughout the Dartmouth College case. By 1820 he was active in Massachusetts politics. He was a Presidential-elector on the Monroe and Tompkins ticket in 1820. Later he served as a Federalist Representative from Massachusetts 1823-1827; United States Senator 1827-1841; Secretary of State 1841-1843; a Whig United States Senator 1845-1850; and Secretary of State 1850-1852.

14. It was stipulated that "if either party should desire it, the statement of facts should be turned into a special verdict, in order that the case might be carried to the Supreme Court of the *United States* upon a writ of error." 1 N. H. 111.

An apocryphal story of this period concerns a plan to strengthen the college's case by bringing from Canada some young Indian students. All went well until the Indians, while crossing the river, saw the stone buildings. At once they dove into the river and fled back north, fearing that they were being taken to prison. IV Beveridge, The Life of John Marshall (1919), 233 note.

15. Shirley, 137-140; Smith, Dartmouth College (1878), 108-112.

16. As a Federalist, he served in Congress from Massachusetts 1811-1814; he was United States Attorney 1814; and Chief Justice of the Superior or Supreme Court of New Hampshire 1816-1838.

17. He had served as a trustee 1808-1811. An Anti-Federalist, he was a member of the New Hampshire State House of Representatives 1804-1807; Speaker 1805-1807; State Senator and President of the Senate 1807-1809; State Councilor 1809-1810; Justice of the Superior Court 1816-1819; Governor 1819-1823; and United States Senator 1823-1835.

18. A doubt has been suggested as to whether Justice Woodbury sat in this case. He had been appointed one of the new trustees of the university in July, 1816, and had attended their meeting of August 26. Later he was appointed a Justice of the Superior Court December 9, 1816, at the age of 28, and took his seat at the February Term, 1817. From 65 N. H. 472, 624, and Farrar's Report of the Dartmouth College Case at pages 28, 206, it appears that "all the judges" were present at the September and November, 1817, Terms. In 1 N. H. 111, there is no express statement as to who participated. However, the local docket for the May and November Terms, 1817, carries a note stating that Justice Woodbury "does not sit" in this case. Shirley, 112, 150-151. Justice Woodbury served on the Superior Court until 1819. An Anti-Federalist, he served later as Governor 1823-1824; State Representative and Speaker 1825; United States Senator 1825-1831; Secretary of the Navy 1831-1834; Secretary of the Treasury 1834-1841; United States Senator 1841-1845; and Associate Justice of the Supreme Court of the United States 1845-1851.

19. The first two had argued the case for the trustees at the May Term, 1817, in Grafton County with Sullivan in opposition. All three had argued for the trustees at the September Term, 1817, at Exeter in Rockingham County, with Sullivan and Bartlett in opposition. With the exception of Webster's, the substance of each of these arguments at Exeter is reported in Farrar, 28-206. The arguments appear also in 65 N. H. 473-624, together

with Farrar's report of Webster's final argument in the Supreme Court of the United States. See Farrar, 238-283.

20. He served as a State Representative in New Hampshire 1805; State Attorney General 1805-1806; in Congress 1811-1813; State Representative and Senator 1813-1815; and State Attorney General 1816-1835.

21. He served as Clerk of the State Senate 1817-1818; a member of the State House of Representatives 1819-1821; and Speaker in 1821. He served as an "Anti-Democrat" in Congress 1823-1829, declined appointment as Chief Justice of the Court of Common Pleas in 1825 and served again in the State House of Representatives 1830, 1838, 1851 and 1852.

22. 1 N. H. 111-138. Reprinted with the addition of arguments of counsel, 65 N. H. 473-643. See also, Farrar, 28-237.

23. 1 N. H. 119-120, 128, 133-134; 65 N. H. 630-631, 636-637, 640.

24. A Federalist, Hopkinson was widely known as the author of "Hail Columbia," written in 1798. He also had a distinguished record at the bar, including his able representation of Justice Samuel Chase in the latter's impeachment trial before the Senate in 1804 and 1805. He served in Congress 1815-1819. From 1828-1842 he was to be a United States District Judge for the Eastern District of Pennsylvania, and in 1837 Chairman of Pennsylvania's Constitutional Convention.

25. He had been a Federalist member of the Massachusetts House of Representatives 1802-1803, then an Anti-Federalist member of the State Senate 1813-1814, and United States Representative 1817-1820. Later he was to serve as United States Senator from Maine 1820-1827, 1829-1833. Still later he was to be a State Representative 1835-1838, and United States Attorney 1841-1843.

26. He was widely known as an author, attorney and orator, who had gained especial fame through his part in the prosecution of Aaron Burr for treason. He had served in the Virginia House of Delegates and in 1816 as United States Attorney. From November, 1817, to 1829, he was Attorney General of the United States. January 31, 1818, he had written to a friend: "I have been up till midnight, at work, every night, and still have my hands full. . . . The Supreme Court is approaching. It will half kill you to hear that it will find me unprepared; but I shall contrive ways and means to keep my professional head, at least, above water." Shirley, 234.

27. "The Honorable, the Chief Justice, and the Associate Justices of the Supreme Court of the United States. Oyez, Oyez, Oyez! All persons having business before the Honorable, the Supreme Court of the United States, are admonished to draw near and give their attention for the Court is now sitting. God save the United States and this Honorable Court." The foregoing is the announcement now used. The date of its origin is uncertain. See also, 2 Warren, The Supreme Court in United States History (rev. ed. 1937), 468-469; Smith, Early Indiana Trials (1858), 137.

28. See statement of Professor Chauncey A. Goodrich, of Yale, who was present at the argument, XV Writings and Speeches of Daniel Webster (1903) 10-13; I Fuess, Daniel Webster (1930), 230-232. Justice Story is

quoted as having said later: "For the first hour, we listened to him with perfect astonishment; for the second hour, with perfect delight; for the third hour, with perfect conviction." Wilson, Daniel Webster and Dartmouth, III The Colophon (1938), 10-11.

29. "Section 10. No State shall . . . pass any Bill of Attainder, ex post facto Law, or Law impairing the Obligation of Contracts, or grant any Title of Nobility."

30. 6 Cranch 87.

31. 7 Cranch 164.

32. Citing *Terrett* v. *Taylor*, 9 Cranch 43, 51-52.

33. There is no stenographic or official report of this peroration. The above version came, unsolicited, to Senator Rufus Choate of Massachusetts, from Chauncey A. Goodrich, Professor of Rhetoric and Oratory at Yale, who, thirty-four years before, at the age of twenty-eight, had gone to Washington especially to hear the case argued. This version reached Senator Choate in time for inclusion in his eulogy of Webster at Dartmouth College July 27, 1853, whence its fame. XV Writings and Speeches of Daniel Webster (1903), 11-13. See also, Wilson, Daniel Webster and Dartmouth, III The Colophon (1938), 7-23. Webster came to regard his argument in this case as the "greatest effort" of his career. I Fuess, Daniel Webster (1930), 245.
In about 1830, Justice Story set down his impression of the same scene. It is on file in manuscript form in the Library of Congress and is published in Wheeler, Daniel Webster, The Expounder of the Constitution (1905), 29-32.

34. Wilson, Daniel Webster and Dartmouth, III The Colophon (1938), 20-22.

35. From the National Intelligencer, quoted in Shirley, 238.

36. Shirley, 238-239.

37. Referring to these copies, Webster had written to Justice Story, "If you send one of them to each of the five judges as you think proper, you will of course do it in a manner least likely to lead to a feeling that any indecorum has been committed by the plaintiffs." Wilson, Daniel Webster and Dartmouth, III The Colophon (1938), 13 note; IV Beveridge, The Life of John Marshall (1919), 257; I Private Correspondence of Webster, 287.

38. An Anti-Federalist, Pinkney had served in Congress in 1791, as Attorney General of Maryland 1805; as Commissioner to London under Jay's Treaty 1796-1804; as Joint Minister to Great Britain with James Monroe 1806-1807; as Minister Plenipotentiary 1807-1811; as Attorney General of the United States 1811-1814; in Congress 1815-1816; and Minister Plenipotentiary to Russia 1816-1818. Later he was to serve as United States Senator December 1819-1822.

39. 4 Wheat. 625, 630-631, 640-641, 643-644, 650, 651-653, 654.

40. Separate opinions by Justices Washington and Story were filed later with the Clerk and are now published with the opinion of the Court.

Justice Johnson concurred, for the reasons stated by the Chief Justice. Justice Livingston concurred, for the reasons stated in the three written opinions. 4 Wheat. 654-713, and see 666. In connection with Story's opinion, see also, his comments in 1833 in *Allen* v. *McKeen*, 1 Sumner 276.

41. The defendant Woodward having died August 9, 1818, the Court, on motion of Webster, entered the order of reversal and remand February 25, 1819, *nunc pro tunc* as of the February Term, 1818.

Justice Story later disposed of the additional cases pending on circuit. The college had won its decision upon a narrower ground than it had originally expected. Counsel's careful preparation and presentation of it had been well rewarded. The trustees, unable to compensate their counsel with substantial fees, voted to have a portrait of each painted by Gilbert Stuart at the college's expense. Today, portraits of Webster, Hopkinson, Mason and Smith, although not by Stuart, are to be seen in Dartmouth Hall. There they constitute a deserved tribute to their subjects and to the principle that whatever is worth doing at all is worth doing well. Lord, History of Dartmouth College (1913), 177-178, 246; I Fuess, Daniel Webster (1930), 224, 243.

PRINCIPAL REFERENCES

The Trustees of Dartmouth College v. *Woodward*, 1 N. H. 111, 65 N. H. 473.

The Trustees of Dartmouth College v. *Woodward*, 4 Wheat. 518.

Fletcher v. *Peck*, 6 Cranch 87.

New Jersey v. *Wilson*, 7 Cranch 164.

IV Beveridge, The Life of John Marshall (1919), 220-281.

Corwin, John Marshall and the Constitution (1921), 147-172.

Farrar, Dartmouth College Case (1819).

I Fuess, Daniel Webster (1930), 215-245.

Lodge, Daniel Webster (1899), 70-106.

Shirley, The Dartmouth College Causes and the Supreme Court (1879).

Smith, The History of Dartmouth College (1878), 100-116.

Warren, An Historical Note on the Dartmouth College Case, 46 Am. L. Rev. 665-675 (1912).

1 Warren, The Supreme Court in United States History (rev. ed. 1937), 475-492.

Webster, The Writings and Speeches of Daniel Webster, 18 Vols. (1903), Peroration in Dartmouth College Case, Vol. 15, 10-13.

Wentworth, Congressional Reminiscences (1882), 39-46.

Wheeler, Daniel Webster, The Expounder of the Constitution (1905), 16-33.

Wilson, Familiar "Small College" Quotations, Daniel Webster and Dartmouth, III The Colophon (1938), 7-23.

Wright, The Contract Clause of the Constitution (1938).

Wright, The Growth of American Constitutional Law (1942), 43-45.

Biographical Directory of the American Congress (1950).

VI

An Independent Judiciary

WHEN YOUNG PEOPLE ask me what the Supreme Court is for, I tell them about a boy who asked me why we had so many courts in Cleveland. In return, I asked him if he played baseball. When he replied, "Of course," I asked him if he used an umpire when he played. To that question, he gave me an answer full of wisdom. He said, "Well, when we want to last a full nine inning game, then we have an umpire." He knew that boys can play a short scrub game without an umpire, but he knew also that if they are to play a long, hard game and not end in a fight, they need an umpire. They do not expect him to be perfect. They expect the umpire to know the rules, to be honest, to apply the rules promptly and, above all, to be independent.

The same is true of life in general. The courts are the umpires. The laws are the rules. In our federal government, our independent judiciary is the keystone that holds in place the other members of the governmental arch which our Constitution has designed to sustain a representative republic, dedicated to the preservation for the individual of the greatest freedom consistent with like freedom for others. With its keystone, an arch has extraordinary strength. Without it, it collapses.

How to secure an independent judiciary? How to assure its continuing independence? The architects of our Constitution solved those major problems by providing that—

1. Federal judges shall be appointed by the President "with the Advice and Consent of the Senate." Art. II, §2.

* Reprinted by permission of the American Bar Association Journal.

They "shall hold their Offices during good Behaviour, and shall, at stated Times, receive for their Services, a Compensation, which shall not be diminished during their Continuance in Office." Art. III, §1. Those provisions reflected lessons learned in the long struggle to free British judges from the domination of their King.[1]

2. All civil officers, including judges, "shall be removed from Office on Impeachment for, and Conviction of, Treason, Bribery, or other high Crimes and Misdemeanors." Art. II, §4. While this provision was primarily for the protection of the public against the abuse of judicial power, an omission was made from the British procedure and a limitation was inserted in the impeachment procedure itself to protect the judges against arbitrary removal from office.

The Constitutional Convention thus omitted a proposed provision to give the President a power of removal comparable to that of the British Crown to remove judges upon a joint address of the Houses of Parliament. Madison's notes tell the story of that omission as follows:[2]

On August 27, 1787, John Dickinson of Delaware moved to insert after the words "good behavior" relating to federal judges, the words "provided that they may be removed by the Executive on the application by the Senate and House of Representatives." Gouverneur Morris of Pennsylvania "thought it a contradiction in terms to say that the Judges should hold their offices during good behavior, and yet be removeable without a trial. Besides it was fundamentally wrong to subject Judges to so arbitrary an authority." Edmund Randolph, of Virginia, "opposed the motion as weakening too much the independence of the Judges."

Eleven states were on the roll call. Of these Massachusetts, New Jersey and North Carolina were absent. Connecticut voted "aye," but Delaware, Georgia, Maryland, New Hampshire, Pennsylvania, South Carolina and Virginia voted "no," and thereby rendered infinite service to the cause of an independent judiciary.

The removal of federal judges was limited also not only to those impeached by the House of Representatives for "Treason, Bribery, or other high Crimes and Misdemeanors" but also to those convicted by the Senate upon the "Concurrence of two thirds of the Members present." Art. I, §3.

The Twelve Impeachment Trials

Under these provisions, the Senate has sat as a Court of Impeachment twelve times. It sat first in 1798 to consider charges against Senator William Blount, of Tennessee. It dismissed them for want of jurisdiction, recognizing that the Constitution authorized each House to be the judge of the qualifications of its own members, to punish them for disorderly behavior and, with the concurrence of two-thirds, to expel a member. Art. I, §5.

Of the other trials, two were of executive officers. One was that of President Andrew Johnson, of Tennessee. He was acquitted in 1868. The other was that of Secretary of War William W. Belknap of Iowa. He resigned before trial and was acquitted in 1876.

The remaining nine were trials of judicial officers, illustrating that the impeachment provisions are applicable especially to offending judges who enjoy substantially life tenure in contrast to the limited tenures of executive officers. Of the judges tried, one was an Associate Justice of the Supreme Court, Samuel Chase, of Maryland. His case will be considered later.

One trial was that of a Circuit Judge for the Third Judicial Circuit, serving on the Commerce Court, Robert W. Archbald, of Pennsylvania. He was removed from office in 1913.

The other seven trials were of District Judges. Of these, Judge George W. English, of Illinois, resigned before trial and his impeachment was dismissed in 1926.

Three judges were acquitted: James H. Peck, of Missouri, in 1831; Charles Swayne, of Florida, in 1905; and Harold Louderback, of California, in 1933. Three were removed from office: John Pickering, of New Hampshire, in 1804; West H. Humphreys, of Tennessee, in 1862; and Halsted L. Ritter, of Florida, in 1936.

Thus, four trials have produced convictions and only those four indicate what the Senate holds to be a sufficient basis for the conviction and removal of a judge. Two of these provide little guidance. Judge Pickering, of New Hampshire, was removed following a substantial concession that he was insane and a recognition that no provision had then been made for terminating his judicial tenure on grounds of disability. Judge Humphreys, of Tennessee, was removed when he adhered to the Confederacy without resigning his federal office. The removal of Judge Archbald in 1913 and that of Judge Ritter in 1936 were, however, upon charges of abuse of their offices for financial gain. In those cases, impeachment, at last, was shown to be an effective, although cumbersome, vehicle in certain circumstances.[3]

The Archbald conviction has now established the jurisdiction of the House to impeach and that of the Senate to convict and remove a judge because of his abuse of judicial authority within the special constitutional meaning of the words "high Crimes and Misdemeanors," although his offenses were not indictable. The Ritter trial demonstrated also that, while a conviction carries with it removal from office, future disqualification to hold office rests in the discretion of the Senate.[4]

The Acquittal of Justice Chase

In the trial of Justice Chase, the controversy was not whether the authority of the Senate was broad enough to reach an abuse of judicial power involving corruption. It was whether the authority of the Senate could, and should, be used to remove a judge because of his procedural rulings, and his statements to a grand jury in criticism of the National Administration. Although the Constitutional Convention had rejected a provision for the removal of a judge upon the application of the Houses of Congress, nevertheless, this proceeding, in substance, was an attempt to reach that result through impeachment by the House and trial by the Senate for alleged high crimes and misdemeanors.

The controversy struck deeper than was apparent. It involved the cleavage between President Jefferson and Chief Justice Marshall as to the latter's doctrine of judicial review of constitutional questions. Until the opinion of the Supreme Court had been announced in *Marbury* v. *Madison*, 1 Cranch 137, the doctrine of final judicial review was not widely understood. After that opinion, Jefferson had little hope of its modification by the Supreme Court which, in 1804, consisted of five Federalists and one Anti-Federalist (William Johnson). If, however, the impeachment and conviction of judges could be made substantially equivalent to their removal upon a joint address of the Houses of Congress, the supremacy of the judiciary would be at the mercy of a majority of the House of Representatives when supported by two-thirds of the members present in the Senate. That road was to be explored.

The events speak for themselves:

February 24, 1803—The opinion in *Marbury* v. *Madison* was announced.

May 2, 1803—Justice Samuel Chase, while on circuit at Baltimore, addressed the grand jury in terms of doubtful propriety understandably offensive to President Jefferson. He said:

> Where law is uncertain, partial, or arbitrary . . . where justice is not impartially administered to all; where property is insecure, and the person is liable to insult and violence without redress by law—the people are *not free*,

[101]

whatever may be their form of government. To this situation I greatly fear we are fast approaching. . . . The late alteration of the Federal judiciary by the abolition of the office of the sixteen circuit judges, and the recent change in our State Constitution by the establishing of universal suffrage, and the further alteration that is contemplated in our State judiciary (if adopted) will in my judgment take away all security for property and personal liberty. The independence of the national judiciary is already shaken to its foundation, and the virtue of the people alone can restore it. . . . Our republican Constitution will sink into a mobocracy—the worst of all possible governments.[5]

This supplemented the Justice's active campaigning in 1800 for the reelection of President John Adams over Jefferson, his long-standing reputation for overbearing manners and his vigorous efforts to enforce the Alien and Sedition Acts which Jefferson abhorred.

May 13, 1803—Jefferson wrote to Representative Joseph H. Nicholson, of Maryland—

You must have heard of the extraordinary charge of Chase to the grand jury at Baltimore. Ought this seditious and official attack on the principles of our Constitution and on the proceedings of a State to go unpunished; and to whom so pointedly as yourself will the public look for the necessary measures? I ask those questions for your consideration; for myself, it is better that I should not interfere.[6]

January 5, 1804—The House of Representatives gave consideration to a motion to appoint a Committee to inquire into the official conduct of Justice Chase and report whether he had so acted as to require the interposition of the constitutional power of the House. Representative John Randolph, of Virginia, Joseph H. Nicholson and others were appointed to that Committee.[7]

March 12, 1804—Following a plea by Judge Pickering's son that his father was insane, the Senate, in the absence of any statutory provision for the judge's retirement for such disability, found him guilty as charged and ordered him removed from office.

On the same day, the House adopted its Committee's Report recommending the impeachment of Justice Samuel Chase for high crimes and misdemeanors.

December 5, 1804—A Committee of seven was appointed to manage the Chase impeachment. It included John Randolph, Caesar A. Rodney, of Delaware, and Joseph H. Nicholson.[8]

December 7, 1804—Having approved eight articles of impeachment, personally drafted by Randolph, the House transmitted them to the Senate.[9] They charged that the Justice—

I. While presiding on circuit in Philadelphia, in April and May, 1800, at the trial of Fries for high treason (1) delivered an opinion on a question of law tending to prejudice the jury against Fries; (2) prohibited counsel for Fries from recurring to certain English authorities and from citing certain statutes of the United States; and (3) debarred counsel for Fries from addressing the jury on the law as well as on the facts of the case.

II. While presiding on circuit in Richmond, also in May, 1800, at the trial of Callender for a criminal libel of President John Adams, had refused to excuse a juror who stated that "he had made up his mind as to the publication from which the words, charged to be libellous . . . were extracted."

III. At the same trial had refused to permit a material witness to testify for Callender "on pretence that the said witness could not prove the truth of the whole of one of the charges contained in the indictment."

IV. During the same trial the Justice's conduct had been marked "by manifest injustice, partiality and intemperance, viz:" (1) in compelling prisoner's counsel to reduce to writing, for their admission or rejection, all questions to be asked of a certain witness; (2) in refusing to postpone the trial because of the absence of a material witness; (3) in using "unusual, rude, and contemptuous expressions towards the prisoner's counsel," and falsely insinuating that such counsel "wished to excite the public fears"; (4) in making repeated and vexatious interruptions of counsel, which induced such counsel to abandon the cause; and (5) in an indecent solicitude for the conviction of the accused.

V. At the same trial had arrested Callender and committed him to close custody, whereas the laws of Virginia prescribed that the court in such a case should order the clerk merely to issue a summons for the accused to appear and make answer.

VI. At the same trial had required the accused to be tried during the term at which he had been indicted, whereas the laws of Virginia prescribed that the accused be held to answer at the next term.

VII. While presiding on circuit in New Castle, Delaware, in June, 1800, after the grand jury had found no bills of indictment, the Justice, nevertheless, had directed the attention of the grand jury to the presence in Wilmington of "a most seditious printer" and had enjoined the district attorney to examine a certain file of papers in order to find in them ground for the prosecution of their printer.

VIII. While presiding on circuit in Baltimore, in May, 1803, in addressing the grand jury, the Justice "did, in a manner highly unwarrantable, endeavor to excite the odium of the said grand jury, and of the good people of Maryland against the government of the United States, by delivering opinions, which, even if the judicial authority were competent to their expression, on a suitable occasion in a proper manner, were at that time and as delivered by him, highly indecent, extra-judicial and tending to prostitute the high judicial character with which he was invested to the low purpose of an electioneering partizan."

December 21, 1804—Senator John Quincy Adams, of Massachusetts, recorded a striking avowal of the purpose of this impeachment, as stated by Anti-Federalist Senator William B. Giles, of Virginia, a leader in the Senate. The avowal was made in a conversation between Senator Giles, Senator Adams, Senator Israel Smith, of Vermont, and Representative John Randolph. Senator Adams' notes recite that—

> Giles labored with excessive earnestness to convince Smith of certain principles, upon which not only Mr. Chase, but all the other Judges of the Supreme Court, excepting the one last appointed [William Johnson, appointed by President Jefferson], must be impeached and removed. He treated with the utmost contempt the idea of an *independent* judiciary—said there was not a word about such an independence in the Constitution, and that their pretensions to it were nothing more nor less than an attempt to establish an aristocratic despotism in themselves. The power of impeachment was given without limitation to the House of Representatives; the power of trying impeachments was given equally without limitation to the Senate; and if the Judges of the Supreme Court should dare, AS THEY HAD DONE, to declare an act of Congress unconstitutional, or to send a mandamus to the Secretary of State, AS THEY HAD DONE, it was the undoubted right of the House of Representatives to impeach them, and of the Senate to remove them, for giving such opinions, however honest or sincere they may have been in entertaining them. . . . I perceive, also, that the impeachment system is to be pursued, and the whole bench of the Supreme Court to be swept away, because *their offices are wanted*. And in the present state of things I am convinced it is as easy for Mr. John Randolph and Mr. Giles to do this as to say it.[10]

January 2, 1805—The stage was set for high drama. The

Senate met in its chamber in the North Building of the Capitol—a rectangular building having neither of the great wings that are now attached to it and having no dome between it and the Hall of the House of Representatives. The chamber was above the ground floor and directly over the courtroom of the Supreme Court.[11] As presiding officer, Vice President Aaron Burr had changed the seating arrangements to conform to those of a court in which the thirty-four Senators were to be the judges.[12] He placed the Senators in equal numbers on his right and left, seated in double straight rows at desks covered with crimson cloth. In front of him sat the Secretary of the Senate and the Sergeants at Arms of the House and Senate. Facing the Court, on the presiding officers' right, was a box for the managers of the House. On his left was another for the accused and his counsel. Both boxes were covered with blue cloth.

At the rear of the semicircular chamber were three benches, rising in tiers, for members of the House, with a box for members of the Executive Department, foreign ministers and others. A temporary gallery, reserved for ladies, had been built above the seats of the House members and beneath the permanent gallery. Those seats and the temporary gallery were covered with green cloth. The public was admitted to the permanent semicircular gallery at the rear.

The procedure resembled that of a court. The Secretary read the return of the summons. Proclamation was made that Samuel Chase either appear or that his default be recorded. He advanced to the center of the chamber and stood there— a signer of the Declaration of Independence, a former outstanding member of the Continental Congress, known as the "Demosthenes of Maryland," a former judge of the Criminal Court of Baltimore, a former chief justice of the General Court of Maryland, an outstanding and vigorous Federalist, and a Justice of the Supreme Court appointed by President Washington in 1796. Sixty-three years old, six feet tall, large of frame, with long white hair, stout, ruddy of complexion, and afflicted with gout, he answered to his name and asked for a chair, which was furnished him. The managers from the House were not present. Justice Chase then rose and made a respectful address, asking for time within which to prepare a detailed answer to the charges against him. He asked that he be allowed until the next session of Congress which, in regular course, would begin December 2, 1805.[13]

January 3, 1805—The constitutionally required oath was administered by the Secretary of the Senate to the Vice President and by the latter to the Senators. The Senate, by a vote of 12 to 18, defeated a motion to set the Justice's answer date as requested on the first Monday in December. By vote of 21 to 9, it set it on February 4, 1805.

February 4, 1805—In the same dramatic setting, the proceedings were resumed.[14] The members of the House, preceded by their Speaker and their seven managers, took their seats.[15] Justice Chase presented his counsel.[16] The reading of Chase's answer by his counsel consumed several hours. The closing portion—in the nature of a religious appeal—was read by the Justice himself.[17]

February 8-20—The Senate met nearly every weekday as a Court of Impeachment. It heard over fifty witnesses.[18] The testimony, in general, substantiated the factual events charged without establishing their illegality, although in some instances indicating their doubtful propriety.

February 20-27—Full arguments were made by both sides. Counsel for the defense were, generally, more impressive than the managers for the House. John Randolph, leader of the managers, who was exhausted by his recent efforts in the Yazoo land scandal debate, suffered by comparison with Joseph Hopkinson and Luther Martin. Counsel for the defense pressed the argument that, under the Constitution, impeachment was and should be limited to indictable crimes and misdemeanors. The House managers, instead of taking a firm position in favor of a broader interpretation, substantially conceded this point, and attempted to bring the articles of impeachment within that interpretation. On Wednesday, February 27, the Senate determined that it would pronounce judgment on Friday, March 1.

March 1, 1805—At twelve thirty, the Vice President was in the chair. All thirty-four Senators were present. Senator Tracy, of Connecticut, had been brought in on a couch but he rose from it and took his regular seat. Nine of the Senators were Federalists. Twenty-five were Anti-Federalists (then generally known as Republicans). As a two-thirds vote of the Senators present was necessary to convict, the vote required to do so was twenty-three. If three Anti-Federalists and the nine Federalists voted "Not guilty," there could be no conviction. The Secretary read the first article—relating to procedure at the Fries trial. He then put the question: *"Is Samuel Chase, esq. guilty or not guilty of a high crime or misdemeanor in the article of impeachment just read?"*[19] Federalist Senator John Quincy Adams, of Massachusetts, was the first called. He voted "Not guilty." The first break came with Senator Bradley, Anti-Federalist Senator from Vermont. He voted "Not guilty." Anti-Federalist Senator Gaillard, of South Carolina, who had entered the Senate January 31 to fill a vacancy, was the next to cross the party line. He voted "Not guilty." The next response was a major surprise. Anti-Federalist Senator Giles, of Virginia, who had championed the broadest possible scope for the Senate's jurisdiction to impeach, voted "Not guilty." When the call was completed, eighteen had voted "Not guilty" and sixteen "Guilty." The prosecution had received two less votes than a plain majority and seven less than the constitutionally required majority of twenty-three.

On the second article, Senator Giles voted "Guilty," and there were several other changes but the total was even more favorable to Justice Chase than on the first. Twenty-four voted "Not guilty"—ten "Guilty."

On the third article—relating to the exclusion of testimony in the *Callender* case—the tide turned slightly. There were sixteen votes of "Not guilty" to eighteen of "Guilty." For the first time, there was a majority for conviction. The vote to convict was, however, still five short of that required.

On the fourth article, the total was the same—sixteen "Not guilty" and eighteen "Guilty."

On the fifth article, in which Justice Chase was charged with arresting Callender instead of summoning him under Virginia practice, the Justice was completely vindicated. The vote was thirty-four "Not guilty."

On the sixth article—in which the Justice was charged with requiring the accused to be tried at the current term instead of at the next term—the Justice's vindication was almost as complete—thirty "Not guilty," and four "Guilty."

On the seventh article—charging that the Justice had improperly instigated the investigation of a seditious printer—the vote was twenty-four "Not guilty" to ten "Guilty."

Finally came the crucial test—the eighth and last article. This charged the offense which had brought on the impeachment—Justice Chase's remarks to the grand jury at Baltimore. Again Senator Bradley, of Vermont, voted "Not guilty." Again Senator Gaillard, of South Carolina, voted "Not guilty." This time, Senator Giles, of Virginia, voted "Guilty." The necessary twelfth vote was not assured until the call reached Anti-Federalist Senator Mitchill, of New York. He recently had come to the Senate from the House of Representatives where, in the preceding year, he had been one of the managers for the House in the impeachment trial of District Judge Pickering. He voted "Not guilty." When the call was completed, there were fifteen votes of "Not guilty" to nineteen of "Guilty." This was the highest total that was reached in favor of the prosecution but it was four below the number required to convict. The independence of the judiciary was saved by that margin. The Constitutional Convention, therefore, should be credited with protecting the independence of the judiciary not only because of the Convention's conscious omission of a provision for the removal of judges upon the joint application of the Houses of Congress but also because of its conscious insertion of a provision requiring the concurrence of two-thirds of the Senators present to convict anyone impeached by the House.

The Vice President announced: *"There not being a constitutional majority on any one article, it becomes my duty to pronounce that Samuel Chase, esq. is acquitted on the articles of impeachment exhibited against him by the house of representatives."* Thereupon, the Court of Impeachment adjourned *sine die*.

The sequel confirmed Senator Adams' analysis of the proceedings. Randolph at once proposed, in the House of Representatives, a constitutional amendment whereby federal judges might be removed on the joint address of the two Houses of Congress.[20] It never has been adopted.

While the grounds for the Senate's acquittal of Justice Chase cannot be determined, it is clear that two-thirds of the Senators were not willing to remove from office a Justice of the Supreme Court on the charges and proof adduced. Some may have voted against removal because they believed that impeachment was not authorized by the Constitution for nonindictable offenses. Others may have voted against removal because, although they believed that some nonindictable offenses were impeachable, yet those charged and proved in this case were not sufficiently serious to come within the kind of "high Crimes and Misdemeanors" that would justify the removal of Justice Chase from office. Still others may have voted against removal simply because the offenses charged were not proved to have been committed.

Since the Archbald and Ritter convictions and removals in

1913 and 1936, it is, however, now reasonable to assume that the Senate recognizes that there are at least some nonindictable offenses that are impeachable and which, if proved, may lead to removal from office. At the same time, the Senate's acquittal of Justice Chase and of other judges has demonstrated that the Senate is reluctant to weaken the independence of the judiciary. There is ground to believe that both the American people and their Senators expect from their courts, no less than from their baseball umpires, honest, informed and independent judgments, regardless of whom the decisions may disappoint.

Our legal profession owes no more sacred obligation than to justify such a faith in the integrity and independence of the judiciary.[21]

NOTES TO CHAPTER VI

1. Originally, the King commissioned his judges to serve during his pleasure—*"durante bene placito."* By the statute of 12 and 13 W. III, c. 2 (1700), it was provided that the tenure of judges be during their good behavior—*"Quamdiu se bene gesserint,* and their Salaries ascertained and established; but upon the Address of both Houses of Parliament it may be lawful to remove them." See also, 1 Blackstone's Commentaries (Lewis' ed. 1902), 267. Nevertheless, by 1776, the King had gained authority to appoint colonial judges to serve at his pleasure, and this was one of the subjects of complaint in our Declaration of Independence. Carpenter, Judicial Tenure in the United States (1918), 2.

2. Documents Illustrative of the Formation of the Union of the American States (1927), 622-623; 2 Farrand, The Records of the Federal Convention of 1787 (1911), 428-429. A right of removal of judges upon the joint address of two Houses of the Legislature exists, however, in several states. Carpenter, *supra*, at 126-135.

3. In The American Commonwealth (1908) at page 211, Bryce refers to impeachment under our Constitution as "the heaviest piece of artillery in the congressional arsenal, but because it is so heavy it is unfit for ordinary use. It is like a hundred-ton gun which needs complex machinery to bring it into position, an enormous charge of powder to fire it, and a large mark to aim at."

4. Proceedings of the United States Senate in the Trial of Impeachment of Halsted L. Ritter, S. Doc. No. 200, 74th Cong., 2d Sess. 639-642 (1936); U. S. Const. Art. I, §3; Art. II, §4.

In 1935, the Senate Rules for Impeachment Trials also were amended so that, upon order of the Senate, its Presiding Officer shall appoint a committee of twelve Senators to receive evidence and take testimony with all the powers of the Senate. Rule XI, Senate Manual (1953), 105.

5. 2 Adams, History of the United States of America During the First Administration of Thomas Jefferson (1898), 148-149.

6. 2 Adams, *supra*, at 150. Nicholson already was one of the managers of the impeachment trial of District Judge Pickering instituted at the suggestion of Jefferson because of the judge's unfitness to perform his duties due to intoxication and other causes. *Id.*, at 143-144.

7. Evans, Report of the Trial of the Hon. Samuel Chase (1805), Introduction, 1, 5. Although Randolph was but thirty years old, he took the lead. He had studied law and was recognized as an effective speaker but had never practiced his profession. This was the same John Randolph, of Roanoke, who three years later, by designation of Chief Justice Marshall, was to serve as foreman of the grand jury that indicted Aaron Burr for treason. See Burton, John Marshall at the Trial of Aaron Burr, 37 A. B. A. J. 735, 786.

8. Evans, *supra*, Introduction, at 12; 1 Warren, The Supreme Court in United States History (rev. ed. 1937), 289.

9. The summaries here presented are made from the articles as reported in Evans, *supra*, Appendix, at 1-6. For Randolph's authorship of the articles, see 1 Memoirs of John Quincy Adams (1874), 364.

10. 1 Memoirs of John Quincy Adams, *supra*, at 322-323.
"It is impossible to put too much emphasis on Giles' avowal. His statement is the key to the Chase impeachment." 3 Beveridge, Life of John Marshall (1919), 159, n. 5. This was the same Senator Giles, who, three years later, upon Aaron Burr's challenge "for favour," withdrew from designation as a member of the grand jury which indicted Burr for treason. See Burton, John Marshall at the Trial of Aaron Burr, *supra*, at 735, 786.

11. About sixty years later, this chamber, in turn, was to begin a service of seventy years as the courtroom of the Supreme Court.

12. Burr came to this session under indictment for the murder of Alexander Hamilton, whom he had killed in a duel less than six months before. This trial was Burr's last substantial service in public office, and it was universally recognized that he presided with marked credit to the Senate and himself. 3 Beveridge, *supra*, at 182-183. For the arrangement of the chamber, see Evans, *supra*, at 1.

13. While the Justice's address was generally restrained and nonprovocative, something of his suppressed feeling appears in the following sentence:
". . . acrimonious as are the terms in which many of the accusations are conceived; harsh and opprobrious as are the epithets wherewith it has been thought proper to assail my name and character, by those who were 'puling in their nurse's arms' [probably referring especially to John Randolph], whilst I was contributing my utmost aid to lay the ground work of American liberty; I yet thank my accusers, whose functions as members of the government of my country I highly respect, for having at length

put their charges into a definite form, susceptible of refutation; and for having thereby afforded me an opportunity of vindicating my innocence, in the face of this honorable court, of my country, and of the world." Evans, *supra*, at 7.

14. February 4, 1805, was the ninth anniversary of the Justice's oath of office as a member of the Supreme Court. Also, on February 4, 1805, the Supreme Court opened its regular February Term. It met and heard arguments from Monday through Saturday throughout the month. Justice Chase sat with it only on February 5 and 6.

15. The managers were Representatives John Randolph, of Virginia; Caesar A. Rodney, of Delaware; Joseph H. Nicholson, of Maryland; Peter Early, of Georgia; John Boyle, of Kentucky; George W. Campbell, of Tennessee; and Christopher Clark, of Virginia.

16. He presented Luther Martin, long Attorney General of Maryland and an acknowledged leader of the American Bar; Robert G. Harper, formerly a leading Federalist member of the House from South Carolina and, subsequently, a Senator from Maryland; and Joseph Hopkinson, of Pennsylvania, well known as the author of "Hail Columbia," later a Federalist Representative from Pennsylvania and finally a United States District Judge. Although not mentioned in the record on this day, his counsel also included Charles Lee, of Virginia, former Attorney General under Presidents Washington and John Adams, and Philip Barton Key, of Maryland, a brother of the author of "The Star Spangled Banner," and himself later to serve as a Federalist Representative from Maryland. 2 Adams, *supra*, at 227 *et seq.;* 1 Memoirs of John Quincy Adams, *supra*, at 355 *et seq.;* Evans, *supra*, at 116 *et seq.*

17. February 7—The Replication of the House was filed and read. February 8—A brief session was held and the examination of witnesses began February 9. During this month, the Senate conducted its legislative work and its consultations in a committee room. It met in legislative session usually at 10:30 A.M. 1 Memoirs of John Quincy Adams, *supra*, at 345-348; Evans, *supra*, Appendix, at 40.

18. Chief Justice John Marshall and his brother William testified on behalf of Justice Chase and were cross-examined. The Chief Justice's testimony related to the Callender trial which had been held in Richmond while Marshall was practicing at that Bar. In that case, he had secured the release of the Sheriff of Henrico County from jury service. On cross-examination, a largely unsuccessful effort was made to obtain from him a criticism of the legality and propriety of Justice Chase's rulings on procedure. Evans, *supra*, at 69-71, and see 64-68.

19. These proceedings are taken from Evans, *supra*, at 268, and the tabulation of votes from the Appendix of that book at 62. Before the first roll call the Vice President ordered the officers in the upper galleries to turn their faces toward the spectators and to seize and commit to prison the first person who should make the smallest noise or disturbance. 1 Memoirs of John Quincy Adams, *supra*, at 362-363, 3 Beveridge, *supra*, at 217-219.

20. 14 Annals of Cong. 1213 (1805). Nicholson added a proposal that State Legislatures might, at will, recall their Senators. *Id.*, at 1214. See also, 15 Annals of Cong. 499-507 (1806).

21. "No conviction is deeper in my mind, than that the maintenance of the judicial power is essential and indispensable to the very being of this government. The Constitution without it would be no constitution; the government, no government." 3 Works of Daniel Webster (6th ed. 1853), 176, and see Haines, The American Doctrine of Judicial Supremacy (2d ed. 1932), 493.

PRINCIPAL REFERENCES

2 Adams, History of the United States During the First Administration of Thomas Jefferson (1898), 143-159, 218-244.

Adams, J. Q., 1 Memoirs of John Quincy Adams (1874).

3 Beveridge, The Life of John Marshall (1919), 157-222.

Campbell, Four Score Forgotten Men (1950), 85-94.

Carpenter, Judicial Tenure in the United States (1918).

Carrington, The Impeachment Trial of Samuel Chase, 9 Va. L. Rev. 485-500 (1923).

Carson, The History of the Supreme Court of the United States (1902), 187-188, 208.

Evans, Report of the Trial of the Hon. Samuel Chase (1805).

2 Farrand, The Records of the Federal Convention of 1787 (1911).

Haines, The Role of the Supreme Court in American Government and Politics, 1789-1835 (1944), 259-265.

Miller, Crisis in Freedom, The Alien and Sedition Acts (1951).

Simpson, Federal Impeachments, 64 Pa. L. Rev. 651-695, 803-830 (1916).

Taft, The Selection and Tenure of Judges, 38 A. B. A. Rep. (1913), 418.

1 Warren, The Supreme Court in United States History (rev. ed. 1937), 269-315.

Biographical Directory of the American Congress (1950).

Congressional Directory, List of Impeachment Trials (1953), 283.

Documents Illustrative of the Formation of the Union of the American States (1927), House Doc. No. 398, 69th Cong., 1st Sess.

VII

Two Significant Decisions

EX PARTE MILLIGAN AND *EX PARTE MC CARDLE**

FOR THIS STORY we turn back the calendar to Monday, March 5, 1866. It is 11 A.M. in the crowded courtroom of the Supreme Court in the Capitol. It is the day set for hearing Case No. 350, *Ex parte Milligan*, with No. 365, *Ex parte Bowles*, and No. 376, *Ex parte Horsey*. The session has just begun. Three attorneys are sworn in as members of the Supreme Court Bar. One of them is among those who will argue for the petitioners in these cases. He is a modest young man of striking appearance, thirty-four years old, six feet tall, powerfully built, and wearing a full brown beard of the cut then often worn by general officers of the Union Army. He is Representative James A. Garfield, of Ohio, and fifteen years later, almost to the day, he will be sworn in as President of the United States.

The cases reflect the passionate conflict of views between the supporters of Lincoln and the Union on one side, and the "Copperheads" of Indiana and neighboring states on the other. The issues are hot from the flames of war. Petitioners Milligan, Bowles and Horsey are civilian citizens of Southern Indiana. A federal military commission has found each of them guilty of conspiring in Indiana, in 1864, against the United States. For this each is serving a life sentence at hard labor.

There is at issue the right of a federal military commission, rather than a civil court and jury, to try such citizens, outside of a combat zone, on charges of subversive acts committed in time of war in a loyal state like Indiana. The case is one of first impression in the Supreme Court. The right of

* Reprinted by permission of the American Bar Association Journal.

the accused to writs of habeas corpus in order to test the validity of their confinement is also at issue.[1]

In the fall of 1864, each petitioner had been arrested in his Indiana home upon the order of Major General Hovey, commanding the Military District of Indiana. Each was charged with (1) conspiracy against the United States; (2) affording aid and comfort against the authority of the United States; (3) inciting insurrection; (4) disloyal practices; and (5) violation of the laws of war. The supporting specifications described the offenses as having been committed largely through or in connection with secret societies known as the "Order of American Knights" or the "Order of the Sons of Liberty."

Petitioners were tried by a specially constituted military commission consisting of a brigadier general, ten colonels and a lieutenant colonel. The trial opened in the courtroom of the Circuit Court of the United States in Indianapolis.[2] Petitioners were represented by their own counsel and the Government by an Army Judge Advocate. Counsel for petitioners made timely but unsuccessful objection to the jurisdiction of the commission and carefully preserved their right to review that question. Petitioners still contend that, whatever may be the merits of the federal charges against them, they are entitled, under the Constitution of the United States, to jury trials by due process of law in the civil courts.

Harrison H. Dodd, the alleged leader of petitioners, was the first to be put on trial by the commission. However, in the midst of that proceeding, he escaped, at night, from his place of confinement in the Post Office Building and fled to Canada. On October 21, 1864, the commission turned to the instant cases. Twenty-five witnesses were used by the prosecution and thirty-six by the defense. Early in the trial, an official of the "American Knights" and "Sons of Liberty" disclosed that he was a United States detective and that he had kept the government well advised of the proceedings and plans of petitioners. With comparable effect, Heffren, who was one of the alleged conspirators, turned state's evidence and the charges against him were dropped. Following completion of the trial, January 1, 1865, the record was sent to Washington for review.

The commission had found Milligan, Bowles and Horsey guilty of every charge and specification and had sentenced each of them to be hanged.[3] The military authorities had noted concurrence. Lincoln made a preliminary examination of the record and returned it for correction. However, before the corrections had been made, Lincoln was assassinated and, on April 15, Johnson succeeded to the Presidency. May 2, he approved the death sentences.

The date of execution was set for May 19. The prisoners were placed in irons. The gallows were erected. The efforts to secure a presidential commutation of the sentence, nevertheless, were doubled. Justice Davis, of the Supreme Court, who long had been convinced of the illegality of comparable commission procedure, asked Governor Morton, of Indiana, to intercede. The Governor did so by letter and personal representative. Mrs. Bowles and others also reached the President. Determined to make treason "odious," he was at first adamant, but became conciliatory as the Confederacy collapsed. On May 10, Jefferson Davis was captured. On May 16, President Johnson commuted Horsey's sentence to life imprisonment and gave Milligan and Bowles respite until June 1.

Milligan prepared a speech for delivery on the scaffold. Bowles wrote his wife that there was no hope. But on May 29 the President issued a proclamation of general amnesty and on May 30 confidentially ordered a commutation of the sentences of Milligan and Bowles to imprisonment at hard labor for life, the announcement to be made on the date set for the execution. That was done on June 2. On June 3 the prisoners were on their way to serve life sentences at the Ohio Penitentiary.[4]

Simultaneously, the litigation now before us had been begun. On May 10, 1865, petitions had been filed in the Federal Circuit Court for the District of Indiana asking for the discharge of Milligan, Bowles and Horsey on the ground of the illegality of their imprisonment by the commission. Motions for writs of habeas corpus were filed with the same court on May 11. That court consisted of Justice David Davis, of the Supreme Court of the United States, sitting as Circuit Justice, and District Judge David McDonald. On May 13 those judges reported themselves to be in opposition to one another in each case on three questions which they certified to the Supreme Court. Those questions, as certified and now pending in the *Milligan* case, are as follows:

> I. On the facts stated in the petition and exhibits, ought a writ of *habeas corpus* to be issued according to the prayer of said petitioner?
> II. On the facts stated in the petition and exhibits, ought the said Milligan to be discharged from custody as in said petition prayed?
> III. Whether, upon the facts stated in the petition and exhibits, the military commission had jurisdiction legally to try and sentence said Milligan in manner and form, as in said petition and exhibit is stated?[5]

While this certificate has postponed the issuance of the writ requested, it has brought with it some important advantages. Assuming that petitioners survive until the questions are answered, the certificate substantially assures a decision by the Supreme Court and it effectively separates the constitutional issues from the emotional handicaps inherent in the offenses.

The parties have agreed, and the Court has ordered, that three counsel may argue for petitioners, three for the government. One more may then close the case for petitioners. Each counsel is allowed three hours.

We pause here for identification of the Court. Four of its Justices antedate, in service, the Presidency of Lincoln. They occupy the seats nearest the Chief Justice. On his right is Justice Wayne, of Georgia, appointed by Jackson thirty-one years ago and now seventy-six years old. On the Chief's left is Justice Nelson, of New York, appointed by Tyler twenty-one years ago. On the right of Wayne is Justice Grier, of Pennsylvania, appointed by Polk nineteen years ago. On the left of Nelson is Justice Clifford, of Maine, appointed by Buchanan eight years ago. The remaining five, all appointed by Lincoln, are Justices Swayne, of Ohio; Miller, of Iowa; on the extreme right, Davis, of Illinois; and on the extreme left, Field, of California. Presiding in the center is the last appointee, Chief Justice Chase, of Ohio, who is beginning his second year on the Court.

In view of the impending developments the following additional facts are noteworthy. Justice Davis was brought to the Court by Lincoln from the Illinois State Circuit where Lincoln had long practiced. Justice Field came to the Court from the Chief Justiceship of the Supreme Court of California but, before moving to California, he had studied law and practiced in partnership with his older brother, David Dudley Field, of New York, who is the leading counsel for petitioners. Chief Justice Chase came to the Court after wide governmental experience as a Senator from Ohio, Governor of Ohio and Secretary of the Treasury in Lincoln's Cabinet.

The cases are called. Joseph Ewing McDonald, of Indiana, opens the argument for petitioners. He is a leader of the Indiana Bar. Formerly a member of Congress and the Attorney General of Indiana, he had, in 1864, defeated petitioner Milligan for the Democratic nomination for Governor only to lose the election to Morton. He reviews fully the preliminary proceedings that have produced the present jurisdictional issues.

Next comes James Abram Garfield, of Hiram, Ohio, recently retired as a major general in the Union Army. His distinguished military record and his standing as a Republican Congressman are calculated to dispose of any suggestion that the case for petitioners rests on partisan premises. He is an effective speaker and, before the war, was president of Hiram College. Since 1863, he has served as a Representative from Ohio and he is destined to continue to serve in Congress or in the Presidency until his assassination in 1881. He makes it clear "that the questions now before this court have relation only to constitutional law, and involve neither the guilt or the innocence of the relators, nor the motives and patriotism of the officers who tried and sentenced them."[6]

He describes the situation in Indiana in 1864 as being 200 miles beyond the sound of a hostile gun, an area never entered by a Rebel foot except on a remote border for one day, and a state where the civil courts were open for business as usual. He contrasts this with an imaginary situation placing Lee and his Army at one end of Pennsylvania Avenue in Washington, with Grant and his Army at the other and approaching the Capitol with roaring guns. In that situation he says: "This court would be silenced by the thunders of war." He analyzes what is meant by martial law and reviews its history. He argues, however, that the mere existence of war and the mere organization of Indiana into a military district is not enough to permit any agency of our government to substitute military commissions for civil courts and thus deprive civilian citizens of trial by jury and due process of law. He also distinguishes the situation in loyal Indiana from that in a hostile state engaged in rebellion.[7]

Garfield is followed by Jeremiah S. Black, of Pennsylvania. Black is an outstanding leader of the American Bar. He has served on the Supreme Court of Pennsylvania and as

Attorney General of the United States. In 1861, he had been nominated by President Buchanan for the Supreme Court and failed of confirmation by a vote of 25 to 26. He served as the official Reporter of the Supreme Court's decisions for its December Terms 1861 and 1862.

He reviews material history and precedents. He traces colorfully the painful development in England of the right of the individual citizen to a trial by jury and to due process of law, in contrast to a trial by any military tribunal under royal command. He calls for the application of all federal constitutional safeguards to civilians in loyal Indiana in 1864. He distinguishes their situation from that of members of the armed forces and that of civilians in occupied territory or in territory within a zone of combat.[8]

The case for the Government is opened by its special counsel, General Benjamin Franklin Butler, of Massachusetts. He has but recently resigned from the army as a major general. He defends the use of military commissions in any state within the military lines of the Union Army and within any theater of military operations. He argues that the fact that civil courts are open is not conclusive that military commissions are unlawful.

After him comes Henry Stanbery, a leader of the Ohio Bar. Next month Stanbery is to be nominated for the Supreme Court only to have the vacancy abolished by Congress. He will then become Attorney General of the United States. He confines his argument largely to objections to the jurisdiction of the Supreme Court to entertain these certified questions under the Judiciary Act of April 29, 1802.[9]

The Government's presentation is concluded by Attorney General James Speed, from Kentucky. He argues for the President's right to use military commissions in time of war by virtue of his authority as Chief Executive and Commander-in-Chief. He supports the President's right to suspend the privilege of the writ of habeas corpus in the interest of public safety and finds congressional justification for that in the Act of March 3, 1863. He claims that even if the military tribunal in 1864 had no jurisdiction to try petitioners, yet these petitioners may now be held as prisoners of war for aiding, with arms, the enemies of the United States. They may be so held, he contends, until the war ends and then handed over to civil authorities.

On March 13, closing the seven days of argument, David Dudley Field, of New York, makes a comprehensive, lucid and exhaustive statement for petitioners. He is at the height of his career as a leader of the American Bar, widely known and highly regarded for his leadership in developing the Legal Code of New York.

He analyzes the issues. He points to the absence of any necessity in Indiana to deny access to civilian courts that are open for business. He emphasizes the fact that the jurisdiction of the commission here at issue rests upon executive rather than congressional authorization. He finds it unnecessary to determine how far the *Congress* lawfully may go in authorizing the use of military commissions.

As to the suspension of the privilege of habeas corpus, he argues that Congress has expressed itself through the Act of March 3, 1863. Under that Act alone, he claims that petitioners are entitled to a writ and to be discharged.

He states the question to be: "Has the President, in time of war, by his own mere will and judgment of the exigency, the power to bring before his military officers any man or woman in the land, to be there subject to trial and punishment, even to death?"[10] He reviews the course of material history and, following his argument, the Court takes the three certified questions under advisement.

Three weeks later, as the term ends on April 3, the Court answers each question in favor of petitioners.[11] On the facts stated in the petitions and exhibits, it states that writs of habeas corpus should be issued, that the prisoners should be discharged from custody and that the military commission had no jurisdiction to try and to sentence petitioners as it did. The victory of petitioners is complete. The men who, a year ago, walked in the shadow of death are alive and soon to be free.[12]

No dissents are noted to the order of April 3, but the Chief Justice announces that the opinion of the Court will be read at the next term "when such of the dissenting judges as see fit to do so will state their ground of dissent."[13]

On December 17, 1866, two weeks after the opening of the next term, the Court's opinion is handed down by Justice Davis. It is followed by a separate opinion in which the Chief Justice is joined by Justices Wayne, Swayne and Miller.[14] It is these opinions that have brought fame to *Ex parte Milligan*. It appears from them that petitioners could be discharged on the narrow ground that the Act of March 3, 1863, requires such a discharge where a grand jury meets as one did in Indianapolis in January, 1865, and adjourns without indicting or filing a presentment against federal prisoners held in custody as were these petitioners. However, the Court does not stop there and, inasmuch as three material questions are certified for its determination, the Court can justify answering each, although the answer to the third may not be essential to the termination of the litigation.

Justices Nelson, Grier, Clifford and Field join Justice Davis in the famous opinion of the Court which considers first the jurisdiction of the commission. It treats that issue as the primary one in the case. If, as they hold, the commission had no jurisdiction to try petitioners, then petitioners are being held in custody without authority and are entitled to prompt discharge for that reason. The opinion goes beyond the facts of the case. It states that *not even Congress* can constitutionally give to a military commission the jurisdiction here sought to be exercised. It is with that statement that Chief Justice Chase particularly disagrees. He does not oppose the discharge of petitioners on other grounds. Furthermore, it is not clear that he differs from the majority in holding that, without legislative support, the President's authorization of a military commission to try these charges is inadequate. In any event, the Chief Justice and those joining his opinion do agree with the majority that the writs of habeas corpus should now be issued and that petitioners should now be discharged from custody.[15] The entire Court distinguishes this case from one concerning hostile occupied territory[16] and from one concerning loyal territory in a combat zone.[17]

This significant decision, exercising the right of final review of the constitutional limitations of executive and legislative authority, has a unique sequel in *Ex parte McCardle*.[18]

The story of this sequel begins on February 5, 1867, when Congress expressly provides for the issuance of writs of habeas corpus by federal courts when persons are restrained of their liberty in violation of the Constitution or of any treaty or law of the United States. The Act also states specifically that appeals may be taken from the Circuit Courts to the Supreme Court in habeas corpus cases.[19] Not long thereafter, McCardle, who is a newspaper editor in Mississippi, is arrested and held for trial before a military commission under one of the Reconstruction Acts. The principal charges against him are libel and those of inciting to insurrection, disorder and violence. Promptly, he petitions a Federal Circuit Court for a writ of habeas corpus under the 1867 Act. When the Circuit Court remands him to military custody, he appeals to the Supreme Court. In January, 1868, his counsel, Jeremiah S. Black, moves for a speedy hearing. The Court, however, puts off the hearing until the first Monday in March, 1868.[20]

Radical Reconstructionists begin to fear that the Court may hold unconstitutional legislation upon which the jurisdiction of the military commission depends. Accordingly, they seek, by legislative action, to avert such a decision. First, they induce the House to pass a bill requiring a two-thirds vote of the Supreme Court to declare any Act unconstitutional. The Senate, however, is not responsive. Next they propose a bill to deprive the Supreme Court of appellate jurisdiction over any case arising out of the Reconstruction Acts. That bill also languishes.

On Monday, March 2, the arguments on the merits of the *McCardle* case begin in the Supreme Court. Because Justice Wayne has died, only eight Justices are present. Six hours are allowed each side. Black and Field speak for McCardle. Senator Lyman Trumbull, of Illinois, and Matthew Hale Carpenter, later to be a Senator from Wisconsin, represent the government. On March 9, the Court takes the case under advisement and seems likely to postpone further action until the next term because Chief Justice Chase has been called from the Supreme Court Bench to preside over the impeachment trial of President Johnson. What the decision would have been on the merits of that case, we shall never know. Watchful of their opportunities, supporters of the Reconstruction program quietly secure the passage in the House of an amendment to an inconspicuous bill. If adopted, that amendment will repeal the appellate jurisdiction of the Supreme Court under the Habeas Corpus Act of 1867, even as to pending cases, and thus deprive the Court of its jurisdiction over the *McCardle* case. The Achilles' heel of the Supreme Court's right of judicial review is thus disclosed. The weakness lies in the fact that the Constitution does not give the Court absolute appellate jurisdiction. The Constitution confers appellate jurisdiction on the Court only "with such Exceptions, and such Regulations as the Congress shall make."[21]

The amendment passes the Senate. President Johnson at once sees in it grave danger of a precedent for congressional manipulation of the Court's jurisdiction. With high courage, in the midst of his own impeachment trial, he vigorously vetoes the bill. This forces the issue into the open, only to have a hostile Senate pass the bill over his veto 33 to 9, with thirteen Senators absent. The House of Representatives follows suit, with a vote of 115 to 57, thus providing a margin of one vote above the constitutionally required two-thirds.

On March 27, eighteen days after the argument of the appeal in the *McCardle* case, the Court's jurisdiction to hear such appeals is thus cut off by Congress.[22] Despite this, Jeremiah Black asks to be heard in opposition to the right of Congress thus to enter the field of pending litigation in a case already submitted to the Court. Following a sharp controversy within the Court, such a hearing is put over until the next term.[23] Final argument is had on March 19, 1869, and, on April 12, the Court unanimously concedes its loss of jurisdiction.[24]

The weakness thus demonstrated in the Court's armor is a matter of continuing concern. To overcome it, the Senate, at a recent session in 1954, included in S. J. Res. 44 a proposal for a constitutional amendment guaranteeing to the Court appellate jurisdiction in all cases arising under the Constitution and limiting to "other cases" the right of Congress to make exceptions to the Court's appellate jurisdiction. The House of Representatives did not vote upon the resolution before adjournment. To be deserving of such confidence is one of the Court's highest responsibilities.

NOTES TO CHAPTER VII

1. Chief Justice Taney, in his individual capacity, in 1861, held unconstitutional President Lincoln's Proclamation suspending the privilege of the writ of habeas corpus but that case did not reach the Supreme Court. *Ex parte Merryman*, Fed. Cas. No. 9,487. In 1864, the Supreme Court decided that it had no power to review by certiorari the proceedings of a military commission, but it did not pass upon the jurisdiction of the commission to try the case. *Ex parte Vallandigham*, 1 Wall. 243.

2. On the tenth day of its session, the commission withdrew from the room where it had been sitting so that the Circuit Court might hold its

regular term there. For the next ten days, the commission occupied the chamber of the Supreme Court of Indiana, but moved from there when the regular term of that court began. Statement by Garfield, quoted in Klaus, American Trials, Ex parte: In the Matter of Lambdin P. Milligan, 118.

3. A fifth defendant, Andrew Humphreys, was found guilty but, as he had not been active in the matters charged, he was sentenced merely to be confined at hard labor during the war and was released on parole. Klaus, *supra,* at 37-38.

4. Following the trial of petitioners by the commission, the Circuit Court had met in Indianapolis. It was attended, January 2, 1865, by a grand jury which adjourned without returning either an indictment or presentment against any of petitioners. Also, no list of persons held as prisoners by authority of the President of the United States or of his Secretary of State or Secretary of War was furnished to the judges of such court. Accordingly, under the terms of the Act of March 3, 1863, 12 Stat. 755, the imprisoned petitioners apparently became entitled to their discharge upon making proper request for it.

5. *Ex parte Milligan,* 4 Wall. 2, 8.

6. Klaus, *supra,* at 94.

7. Something of the spirit of the hearing can be gathered from Garfield's following summary:

"Your decision will mark an era in American history. The just and final settlement of this great question will take a high place among the great achievements which have immortalized this decade. It will establish forever this truth, of inestimable value to us and to mankind, that a republic can wield the vast enginery of war without breaking down the safeguards of liberty; can suppress insurrection, and put down rebellion, however formidable, without destroying the bulwarks of law; can, by the might of its armed millions, preserve and defend both nationality and liberty. Victories on the field were of priceless value, for they plucked the life of the republic out of the hands of its enemies; but

'Peace hath her victories
No less renowned than war.'

and if the protection of law shall, by your decision, be extended over every acre of our peaceful territory, you will have rendered the great decision of the century." Klaus, *supra,* at 119.

8. In eulogizing this address, Representative Maish, of Pennsylvania, later said: "Freedom was his client. The great cause of Constitutional Liberty hung upon that single life." Quoted by Clayton in Reminiscences of Jeremiah Sullivan Black (1887), 132.

9. 2 Stat. 159.

10. Klaus, *supra,* at 169.

11. 4 Wall. 2, 107, and see 3 Wall. 776.

12. April 10, at 3 P.M., the warden releases Milligan on a writ of habeas corpus. By 5 P.M., the warden has received word that the President has

remitted the sentences and ordered the discharge of all three petitioners. He then releases Bowles and Horsey.

June 8, 1865, indictments for conspiracy had been filed against Dodd, Milligan, Bowles and other leaders of the Sons of Liberty. However, these are never pressed to trial and, in 1867, they are nolled. Klaus, *supra*, at 42, 44-45.

13. 18 L. Ed. 291.

14. The minutes of the Court state that "Mr. Chief Justice Chase delivered an opinion concurred in by Mr. Justices Wayne, Swayne and Miller dissenting on third question certified."

15. About two years later, Milligan sued Major General Hovey, the members of the commission and others. The case, alleging wrongful arrest and imprisonment, was tried in the Federal Circuit Court for the District of Indiana. Milligan was represented by Senator, later Vice President, T. A. Hendricks, of Indiana. The defendants were represented by Brigadier General, later President, Benjamin Harrison, also of Indiana. Circuit Judge Drummond charged the jury that Milligan was entitled to recover compensatory damages, but only for the imprisonment suffered within two years before the commencement of the action. This left about one month to be considered and the jury awarded Milligan $5. *Milligan* v. *Hovey*, Fed. Cas. No. 9,605, and see Klaus, *supra*, at 45. See also, *McCormick* v. *Humphrey*, 27 Ind. 144.

16. See *Madsen* v. *Kinsella*, 343 U. S. 341.

17. See *Duncan* v. *Kahanamoku*, 327 U. S. 304.

18. 7 Wall. 506. Justice Wayne died in 1867, leaving a court of eight members to hear and decide this case.

19. 14 Stat. 385.

20. In the meantime, Black successfully resists a motion to dismiss the appeal as not covered by the Act of 1867. *Ex parte McCardle*, 6 Wall. 318.

21. Art. III, §2.

22. 15 Stat. 44. Section 2 provides "That so much of the act approved February 5, 1867 . . . as authorizes an appeal from the judgment of the circuit court to the Supreme Court of the United States, or the exercise of any such jurisdiction by said Supreme Court on appeals which have been or may hereafter be taken, be, and the same is, hereby repealed."

23. 2 Warren, The Supreme Court in United States History (rev. ed., 1937), 482.

24. 7 Wall. 506. See also, Martig, Congress and the Appellate Jurisdiction of the Supreme Court, 34 Mich. L. Rev. 650.

PRINCIPAL REFERENCES

Ex parte Vallandigham, 1 Wall. 243.

Ex parte Milligan, 4 Wall. 2, and see 3 Wall. 776.

Ex parte McCardle, 7 Wall. 506, and see 6 Wall. 318.

Duncan v. *Kahanamoku*, 327 U. S. 304.

Madsen v. *Kinsella*, 343 U. S. 341.

Ex parte Merryman, Fed. Cas. No. 9,487.

Milligan v. *Hovey*, Fed. Cas. No. 9,605.

Habeas Corpus Act of March 3, 1863, 12 Stat. 755.

Suspension of Habeas Corpus, Proclamation of September 15, 1863, 13 Stat. 734.

Habeas Corpus Act of February 5, 1867, 14 Stat. 385.

Repeal of Right of Appeal to Supreme Court in Habeas Corpus Cases, 15 Stat. 44.

Clayton, Reminiscences of Jeremiah Sullivan Black (1887), 126-134.

Fairman, Mr. Justice Miller and the Supreme Court (1939), 84-89, 90-97.

Fesler, Secret Political Societies in the North During the Civil War (1918), 14 Ind. Magazine of History, 224-269.

Foster, The Suspension of the Writ of Habeas Corpus (1918), 3 Va. L. Reg. (N. S.) 665-672.

1 Foulke, Life of Oliver P. Morton (1899), 387-432.

Hart, Salmon Portland Chase (1899), 342-346.

Hughes, War Powers Under the Constitution, A. B. A. Annual Meeting (1917), S. Doc. No. 105, 65th Cong., 1st Sess. 11-12.

Hughes, The Supreme Court of the United States (1927), 108-110.

Klaus, American Trials, Ex parte: In the Matter of Lambdin P. Milligan (1929).

Milton, Abraham Lincoln and the Fifth Column (1942), 240-322.

2 Warren, The Supreme Court in United States History (rev. ed., 1937), 364-374, 418-497.

Wyzanski, The Writ of Habeas Corpus, 243 Annals Am. Acad. Pol. & Soc. Sci. (1946), 101 106.

Biographical Directory of the American Congress (1950).

2 Dictionary of American Biography (1929).

VIII

John Marshall: The Man*

"IGHLY AS HE was respected, he had the rare happiness to be yet more beloved."[1] This was said of the late John Marshall, in 1835, in his home city of Richmond, Virginia, by the Bar and officers of the Circuit Court over which he had presided as a Circuit Justice for more than a generation.

Best known today for his creative opinions interpreting the Constitution of the United States as endowing the federal government with powers adequate for its effective operation, Chief Justice Marshall also was a vigorous, courageous, warm-hearted and modest man, exemplifying the best traditions of the American Revolution.

Born in Virginia, on September 24, 1755, he was the oldest of fifteen children, nine boys and six girls. Raised among the Blue Ridge Mountains, he received his early education from local clergymen and his parents. John's father, Thomas Marshall, built a home at Oak Hill, and was one of the original subscribers to the first American publication of Blackstone's Commentaries. Thomas Marshall served in the Virginia House of Burgesses, at Williamsburg, was Sheriff of Fauquier County and later Clerk of Dunmore County. At nineteen, John was six feet tall, straight and slender, with thick black hair and penetrating dark eyes.

He became a soldier of distinction. At nineteen, he was a lieutenant commanding Virginia "Minute Men" fighting British Grenadiers near Norfolk. In March, 1776, he was a lieutenant in the Third Virginia Regiment in which his father was a major. Joining Washington's army, John took part in the engagements at Iron Hill, Brandywine and Germantown.

* Reprinted by permission of the University of Pennsylvania Law Review.

At Valley Forge he shared the hunger and cold which tested America's fortitude and devotion. "[N]othing discouraged, nothing disturbed" John Marshall.[2] A champion at quoits, and generally a leader in athletic contests, he was nicknamed "Silver Heels" because of the white yarn that his mother had knitted into the heels of the woolen stockings in which he won many foot races. Later he fought at Monmouth, Stony Point, and elsewhere. Soon promoted to a captaincy, he was, by 1793, commissioned a brigadier general in the Virginia militia. In that capacity he commanded a brigade in the Whiskey Rebellion and, until appointed Chief Justice, he usually was addressed as General Marshall.

John had little formal legal education. He attended but six weeks of law lectures by George Wythe at William and Mary College, where he was a member of the debating team of Phi Beta Kappa. At Valley Forge he had served as a Deputy Judge Advocate. When twenty-five, he received from his cousin, Thomas Jefferson, then Governor of Virginia, a license to practice law and was admitted to the Bar in Fauquier County in 1780. In 1782, he was elected to the Virginia House of Delegates and then to the council of eight members chosen by joint ballot of the two Houses of the Assembly.

Eight times he was sent to the Assembly. When the new Federal Constitution was referred to the States for ratification, he urged that Virginia call a convention to act upon it. Such a convention met in 1788, with Marshall a member of it. His service to the Constitution dates from that time. In the convention he directed his principal attention to taxation, the militia and the judiciary, and stoutly supported ratification of the Constitution as a whole. This vital approval was secured by the narrow margin of ten votes.

While Marshall accepted these calls to public service, he declined others. In 1789, although named by President Washington as District Attorney of the United States at

Richmond, he declined the nomination. The same was true when Washington offered him the Attorney Generalship of the United States in 1795, and the post of Minister to France in 1796. However, in 1797, when the need was pressing, President Adams induced him to join C. C. Pinckney and Elbridge Gerry on the XYZ Commission that attempted to adjust international differences with France in the days of Talleyrand. In that capacity he rendered high diplomatic service with widely commended integrity and skill. Throughout these years he was an active proponent of Washington's policies, although many Virginians were turning to the anti-Federalist leadership of Thomas Jefferson.

In 1798 he declined an appointment to the Supreme Court of the United States to succeed Associate Justice Wilson.[3] But in the same year, at the urgent request of George Washington, he ran for Congress from the Richmond District. He made a vigorous campaign. Unlike many Federalist candidates, he declared himself against the revival of the Alien and Sedition Laws, and, with the support of Patrick Henry, was elected, in April, 1799, to the Sixth Congress by 108 votes. Congress convened in Philadelphia, December 2, and on December 18 Marshall performed the painful duty of announcing the death of Washington. On December 19 he offered the resolutions, drafted by "Light-Horse Harry" Lee, which described Washington as "first in war, first in peace, and first in the hearts of his countrymen." These were precisely the sentiments of John Marshall.

In Congress he pursued an independent course. He cast a crucial vote, against his party, for the repeal of the most hotly contested section of the Sedition Law. He killed a Disputed Elections Bill that would have benefited the Federalists in the next presidential election. On the other hand, he ably defended the Jay Treaty and the Administration's conduct in a *cause célèbre* as to an alleged mutineer who had been handed over to a British Consul.

On May 12, 1800, President Adams named him Secretary of State and in June he resigned from Congress to assume his duties in the Cabinet. He declined to use his influence in favor of either side in the contest between Jefferson and Burr which resulted, on February 17, 1801, in the election by the House of Representatives of Jefferson as President and Burr as Vice President. He performed his duties as Secretary of State until late on March 3, 1801, although he had been appointed Chief Justice in January and had been sworn in as such February 4, 1801. On March 4 he administered the presidential oath of office to Jefferson.

Marshall's appointment to the Court terminated most of his activities in other governmental fields. To this there was one notable exception. In 1829, together with former Presidents Madison and Monroe, he accepted election to the Virginia Convention called to revise the Constitution of that Commonwealth. As a member of its Judiciary Committee, he helped to secure provisions for an independent judiciary.

The above activities would have constituted a full career for most men but in Marshall's case, his judicial career became so extraordinary that his earlier services are but little known. They are important, however, not only on their own account but also because they help to explain the breadth of his understanding of constitutional issues.

In the legal profession, he was the leader of his local Bar as a trial lawyer. In 1786 his standing was such that when Edmund Randolph was elected Governor of Virginia, Marshall took over his practice. In May of that year, Marshall's name first appeared in the Reports of the Court of Appeals of Virginia.[4] In about 1793, with the help of Robert Morris of Philadelphia, he and several associates contracted to buy the remaining Fairfax estates of over 160,000 acres in Virginia. This was his greatest financial undertaking. It caused him much anxiety but yielded substantial returns. In 1796 he made an impressive but unsuccessful argument in the Supreme Court of the United States.[5]

A disciple of George Washington, he undertook, while Chief Justice, to write a biography of Washington after the latter's death. It was primarily a labor of love and an expression of loyalty to Washington. Forced to early publication between 1802 and 1804, its five volumes contained valuable historical material, but were neither a financial nor a literary success. Many years later, he shortened the work to three volumes. One was published as a preliminary history of the colonial period and the other two as a "Life of Washington." These were better received. Today they help to confirm the thesis that Marshall, to a substantial degree, succeeded to Washington's leadership in the establishment of a strong, representative federal republic dedicated to the preservation for the individual of the greatest freedom consistent with like freedom for all.

While Marshall's judicial career requires separate treatment for adequate demonstration of its monumental character, some reference to it is essential in any biographical sketch of him. He served as Chief Justice from 1801 to 1835. Such service is longer than that of any other Chief Justice of the United States, and all of it was rendered during the crucial formative period of the nation's history. Under his leadership, the loose stones provided for the nation's structure were built into a firm foundation.

While best known for the opinions he wrote for the Court in the exercise of its appellate jurisdiction, he also rendered outstanding service as a Circuit Justice. The most famous of his circuit cases was the trial and acquittal, in 1807, of Aaron Burr on a charge of treason.[6] Marshall's conduct in this case set an admirable example of judicial courage and demeanor.

While he was a member of the Supreme Court, it decided sixty-two cases on questions of constitutional law. In these he wrote thirty-six opinions for the Court. These are the foundation stones of our constitutional law upon which his fame and much of the stability of our federal structure depend.[7] In appraising this contribution and Marshall's part in it, it is important to emphasize the fact that these decisions were not his alone. However, to him as Chief Justice and author, there must go substantial credit for securing the support of a majority of the Court. Twenty-three of the decisions were unanimous. To appreciate this phase of his service, we should see him as the leader of those able judges who constituted "the Marshall Court." Together, they made, nurtured and protected great precedents. Chief Justice Marshall served with fifteen Associate Justices. Seven were with him many years. They were: Thompson for twelve years, Livingston for sixteen, Todd for nineteen, Story for twenty-three, Duvall for twenty-three, Washington for twenty-nine and William Johnson for thirty years. There has been no other period of comparable continuity, and none when continuity was so essential.

Returning to Marshall the man, he was a devoted husband and father. Brought up in a large family, he treasured family associations. On January 3, 1783, he married "Polly" Ambler, one of four sisters of a distinguished Virginia family. She was not quite seventeen and he was twenty-seven. He had been in love with her for three years, since, as a young Army officer, he first saw her in Yorktown. They had ten children, six of whom survived to maturity, five sons and one daughter. Although obliged to spend much time in Washington, he delighted to return to his home in Richmond. There he lived in the Georgian style brick house which he built on a two-acre plot. He was deeply affected when his wife died on Christmas Day, 1831. Thereafter, he constantly wore, on a chain around his neck, a locket containing a lock of her hair. He, himself, underwent a serious operation in 1831 but regained his health and lived until July 6, 1835.

The famous Liberty Bell that rang in Philadelphia in 1776 to announce the Declaration of Independence tolled to announce his death. His active service and that of the bell ended together, for, as the bell tolled, it cracked. Their voices were silenced but they have never ceased to inspire the nation to seek to fulfill the high mission to which both Marshall and the bell were dedicated.

Marshall's judicial service is fittingly recognized in the excellent bronze statue of him, which faces the sunset on the lower west terrace of the Capitol. Appropriately placed near where Marshall presided over the Court, this statue is the work of W. W. Story, a son of the Chief Justice's friend and colleague, Associate Justice Story. It represents the Chief Justice, sitting in his judicial robe, expounding upon some subject of deep interest to him as he looks toward the towering monument erected to the memory of Washington, whom he so greatly admired.

In keeping with Marshall's devotion to his wife, his body is buried beside hers in Richmond. And in keeping with his modesty, the following simple inscriptions, written by him, appear on horizontal tablets above the graves. On his, we read: "John Marshall, Son of Thomas and Mary Marshall, was born the 24th of September, 1755. Intermarried with Mary Willis Ambler, the 3d of January, 1783. Departed this life the [6th] day of July, 1835." On hers: "Sacred to the memory of Mrs. Mary Willis Marshall, Consort of John Marshall, Born the 13th of March, 1766. Departed this life the 25th of December, 1831. This stone is devoted to her memory by him who best knew her worth, And most deplores her loss."

NOTES TO CHAPTER VIII

1. Brockenbraugh, Reports of Cases Decided by John Marshall in the Circuit Court of the United States (1837), xviii. This phrase is quoted also in Thayer, John Marshall (1901), 155-156.

2. Lieutenant Slaughter said this of him at Valley Forge, as quoted in I Beveridge, The Life of John Marshall (1916), 118.

3. George Washington's nephew, Bushrod Washington, received the appointment and later served on the Court nearly twenty-nine years with Marshall.

4. As counsel in *Hite* v. *Fairfax*, 4 Call 42, 69. This was the first of more than 120 cases which he argued in that court.

5. As counsel in *Ware* v. *Hylton*, 3 Dall. 199, 210.

6. *United States* v. *Burr*, 25 Fed. Cas. Nos. 14,692a-14,694a.

7. See *Marbury* v. *Madison*, 1 Cranch 137 (1803); *Fletcher* v. *Peck*, 6 Cranch 87 (1810); *Sturges* v. *Crowninshield*, 4 Wheat. 122 (1819); *M'Culloch* v. *Maryland*, 4 Wheat. 316 (1819); *Dartmouth College* v. *Woodward*, 4 Wheat. 518 (1819); *Cohens* v. *Virginia*, 6 Wheat. 264 (1812); *Gibbons* v. *Ogden*, 9 Wheat. 1 (1824); *Ogden* v. *Saunders*, 12 Wheat. 213 (1827); *Brown* v. *Maryland*, 12 Wheat. 419 (1827).

IX

The *Legal Tender* Cases

A CELEBRATED SUPREME COURT REVERSAL*

OF THE MANY controversies engendered by the *Legal Tender* cases,[1] those relating to the following propositions are especially provocative:

1. The justification, as a matter of national policy, of the Legal Tender Act of February 25, 1862,[2] declaring Treasury notes of the United States legal tender for the payment of public and private debts.

2. The justification, as a matter of law, of the decision by the Supreme Court made on February 7, 1870, that such declaration was unconstitutional, at least in its application to debts incurred before the passage of the Act.

3. The wisdom of announcing that decision when, with two vacancies on the Court, the decision was supported by four Justices and opposed by three.

4. The propriety of appointing Justices Strong and Bradley to fill those vacancies.

5. The wisdom of the Court's order, made in another case on April 1, 1870, that the whole Court reconsider the above issue of constitutional law decided on February 7, 1870.

6. The justification, as a matter of law, of the Court's decision, made by a majority of five to four, in 1871, reversing its decision of 1870 and holding the Legal Tender Act constitutional in its application to debts incurred before, as well as to those incurred after, the effective date of the Act.

This article deals with the third and fifth controversies.[3] They relate to the announcement of the four-to-three decision against the constitutionality of the Act and the re-

* Reprinted by permission of the American Bar Association Journal.

consideration, within eight weeks, of the same issue by the same Justices plus the two newly appointed members of the Court.

To appreciate the difficulties facing the Court, it is necessary to understand the extraordinary conjunction of circumstances in which the Court found itself. The nation was in a postwar economic crisis. The air was charged with political and sectional emotions. Feelings aroused by the war, the assassination of Lincoln, the Reconstruction Program, and the impeachment trial of Johnson were hot. Congress recently had abruptly deprived the Court of its jurisdiction to decide a pending appeal involving the validity of a Reconstruction Act.[4] In 1866, in order to forestall appointments to the Court by President Johnson, Congress had prescribed that no Associate Justice be appointed until, by death or resignation, the number of Associate Justices had dropped from nine to six.[5] More recently, in 1869, after President Johnson was out of office, Congress had increased the authorized number of Associate Justices to eight.[6] The resulting vacancy and the one to be caused by the resignation of Justice Grier were unfilled on February 7, 1870.

The issue of the validity of the Legal Tender Act was overlaid with prejudices and convictions rooted in the recent war. Many regarded it as a measure which had been adopted only *in extremis* to prevent an impending collapse of the war effort. Salmon P. Chase, as Secretary of the Treasury, originally had doubted its constitutionality and wisdom. When overruled by President Lincoln, he had, nevertheless, supported it as a necessary war measure.[7] Thus supported, the Act had been passed, the greenbacks issued and the nation's currency depreciated. Until 1865, the constitutionality of the measure had been sustained wherever tested in the state courts. However, in that year, the Court of Appeals of Kentucky held to the contrary in *Griswold* v. *Hepburn*.[8] In December, 1867, that case was argued before the Supreme Court of the United States. It was reargued in December, 1868, and, on February 7, 1870, the decision of the Kentucky court was affirmed. That decision, made by a vote of four Justices to three, occasioned widespread surprise. The surprise was due not only to the prior state court decisions to the contrary but also to the fact that the former Secretary of the Treasury, who had supported the measure on its passage, had, since December 15, 1864, been Chief Justice of the Court and had now decided against the constitutionality of the application of the Act, at least to debts incurred before its passage. Moreover, the Supreme Court itself had not previously intimated that it doubted the validity of the Act and it had been widely relied upon by the public for eight years.[9]

The situation within the Supreme Court was complicated by the Act of April 10, 1869. That Act had increased the number of authorized Associate Justices from the existing seven to eight, effective on the first Monday in December. On December 14, President Grant had nominated his Attorney General, Ebenezer Rockwood Hoar, of Massachusetts, to the new vacancy but opposition developed to his confirmation and his name was rejected on February 3, 1870.[10]

Justice Grier's failing health introduced another difficulty. He was in his seventy-sixth year but felt that he could not afford to resign in the absence of an adequate pension. The Act of April 10, 1869,[11] also effective in December, 1869, met this need by permitting a federal judge, who had at least ten years of service and had reached the age of seventy, to resign and receive full pay for the balance of his life. Accordingly, Justice Grier, on December 15, resigned, making his resignation effective February 1, 1870.[12] To fill his place, President Grant nominated Lincoln's famous Secretary of War, Edwin M. Stanton, of Pennsylvania. The nomination was made on Stanton's fifty-fifth birthday, December 19. The next day it was confirmed by the Senate but, on December 24, he died.

Again confronted with two vacancies, the President, at noon, Monday, February 7, 1870, sent to the Senate his nominations of Judge William Strong, of the Supreme Court of Pennsylvania, and Joseph P. Bradley, a leader of the Bar in New Jersey. Strong was confirmed on February 18, took office on March 14, and was assigned as the Circuit Justice of Grier's former Circuit—the Third. Bradley became the additional Justice, in effect succeeding to the place vacated by Justice Wayne, of Georgia, in 1867. Bradley was confirmed March 21, took office March 23, and was assigned to the Southern Circuit—the Fifth.

The *Legal Tender* cases, in 1869, were thus in the center of a kaleidoscopic action. It appears that they were considered by the Court in conference November 27 and that, after discussion of the *Hepburn* case, a vote was taken on it. The result was: For affirmance, Chief Justice Chase, Justices Nelson, Clifford and Field. For reversal, Justices Grier, Swayne, Miller and Davis. That result, if announced, would have produced a decision by an evenly divided Court, and, without written opinion, would have affirmed the Kentucky judgment which invalidated the Act, contrary to the final judgments of several other states sustaining the Act.

The conference, it is reported, then proceeded to consider the comparable companion case of *Broderick's Executor* v. *Magraw*.[13] In that discussion, Justice Grier took a position somewhat inconsistent with his vote in the *Hepburn* case. When this was demonstrated, he changed his position in the *Hepburn* case which made the vote five to three for affirmance in each case.

There yet remained to be decided the question of policy whether to announce this result or to await the participation of a full Court after further reargument. Only if Justice Grier's final vote were fully expressive of his considered judgment, and only if the Court's action were announced before his resignation took effect, would it meet the requirements of the salutary practice of the Court which had been approved by Chief Justice Marshall in *Briscoe* v. *Bank of Kentucky*[14] when the authorized membership of the Court was seven. He there said:

> The practice of this court is, not (except in cases of absolute necessity) to deliver any judgment in cases where constitutional questions are involved, unless four judges concur in opinion, thus making the decision that of a majority of the whole court. In the present cases four judges do not concur in opinion as to the constitutional questions which have been argued. The court therefore direct these cases to be reargued at the next term, under the expectation that a larger number of the judges may then be present.

Justices Swayne, Miller and Davis sought to withhold the announcement of any decision until after reargument before a full Court of nine members. The other five Justices declined to do so and the Chief Justice proceeded to prepare an opinion for the Court. On Saturday, January 29, he read the proposed opinion to the conference and received approval of it from Justices Grier, Nelson, Clifford and Field. Justice Miller, however, asked for time to prepare a dissent. Announcement of the decision, accordingly, was postponed from Monday, January 31, to Monday, February 7. In the meantime, Justice Grier's resignation took effect so that the decision, when announced, had the support of only four sitting Justices and the opposition of three, on a Court with two vacancies. Seeking to offset this, the Chief Justice announced that Justice Grier had concurred in the opinion before Grier's resignation had taken effect.[15]

The result was that, although the decision carried a bare majority of the seven Justices participating, it did not carry with it a majority of the whole membership of the Court authorized by Congress and about to be filled. While, technically, this shortage would not have been so had the decision been announced January 31, the substance of the situation would have been much the same. The need in such a case is for a decision carrying not merely a fleeting majority of the whole Court, but for one carrying reasonable assurance of the support of such a majority for a substantial period. In the absence of some more compelling necessity than existed here, the greater stability inherent in a fully considered decision of a majority of the whole Court justifies adherence to the practice announced by Chief Justice Marshall.

Many considerations support that practice. It promotes stability of decision because, as long as no change occurs in the membership of the majority which has made a decision, it is not likely that any one of that majority will change his position. Also, the requirement of a concurrence of a greater number in the decision is some added assurance of its soundness. On the other hand, the difficulty of overcoming a decision of the Supreme Court on constitutional law by the adoption of a constitutional amendment is great. Accordingly, under some circumstances, that difficulty may justify the Court, as a whole, in reversing or modifying its own decisions. Generally, however, that very difficulty of amendment only emphasizes the importance of the Court giving such careful consideration to its initial decision that no reversal of it shall be needed. For these reasons, the additional degrees of stability and soundness inherent in the concurrence of a majority of the whole Court, as against a lesser majority, usually outweigh whatever delay or inconvenience may be incident to securing the agreement of a majority of the whole Court upon any issue of constitutional law.

After the above-stated four-to-three decision had been announced on February 7, 1870, further procedure became even more difficult. Cases involving related issues, including that of the application of the Act to debts incurred after its passage, were pending and ready for consideration. The reasoning behind the Court's opinion in the *Hepburn* case apparently required holding the Act invalid as to debts incurred after, as well as before, its passage. The three minority Justices strongly opposed such a proposed extension of the *Hepburn* decision. The two new Justices wished to hear argument. Together with the original three dissenters, this produced a majority of five to four in favor of a motion of the Attorney General of the United States to open the argument on such pending appeals so as to embrace all material constitutional issues.

The controversy over the reopening of the case was as sharp as that over the decision in the *Hepburn* case itself. There arose a difference of opinion, within the Court, as to whether an oral understanding previously had been reached that the decision in the *Hepburn* case would be binding in these cases. Both sides were adamant. Accordingly, the pending appeals were set for argument, including their constitutional issues. On the hearing day, the appellants, in open court, moved to dismiss their own appeals and thus to preclude the reopening of the constitutional issues. The Attorney General objected and the Court, at the request of Justice Miller, withdrew to consider the motion. On April 20, the Court announced that the appellants had a right to dismiss their appeals and thus, temporarily, the controversy was stilled.[16]

The intensity of the conflict within the Court, in which Justice Miller led the opposition to the Chief Justice, is indicated in the following letter he wrote to his brother-in-law on April 21:

> We have had a desperate struggle in the secret conference of the court for three weeks over two cases involving the legal tender question. The Chief Justice has resorted to all the stratagems of the lowest political trickery to prevent their being heard, and the fight has been bitter in the conference room. Finally the new judges and the minority in Hepburn v. Griswold having withstood

all assaults public and private, when the cases were called for argument yesterday, the Appellants dismissed their appeal. No doubt they had been paid to do it as their claims were not large and a decision in their favor hardly probable.

The excitement has nearly used me up. It has been fearful; and my own position as leader in marshalling my forces, and keeping up their courage, against a domineering Chief, and a party in court who have been accustomed to carry everything their own way, has been such a strain on my brain and nervous system as I never wish to encounter again.[17]

This was but a skirmish before the final engagement. On April 30, the pending Texas cases of *Knox* v. *Lee* and *Parker* v. *Davis*,[18] raising the constitutional issue both as to prior and subsequent debts, were ordered reargued at the next term of Court. Elaborate reargument was had. On May 1, 1871, a judgment was announced holding the Legal Tender Act constitutional as to contracts whether made before or since its passage. Publication of all opinions was deferred until January 15, 1872. The Court's opinion was written by Justice Strong, with a concurring opinion by Justice Bradley. Justices Swayne, Miller and Davis joined in the opinion of the Court. Chief Justice Chase wrote the principal dissenting opinion. In this he was joined by Justices Clifford and Field, each of whom also wrote a separate dissent. Justice Nelson noted his dissent. The reported case covers 224 pages.[19]

Thus, within fifteen months, the Court reversed its own four-to-three decision by a five-to-four decision on a matter of fundamental law and of widespread practical concern to the nation and to its individual citizens. This result has been classed by Chief Justice Hughes with the *Dred Scott* case[20] and the *Income Tax* case[21] as one of "three notable instances [in which] the Court has suffered severely from self-inflicted wounds."[22] It has been contended that the infliction of this wound should have been prevented by the Court's refusal to reopen the case once it had been decided. It is more probable, however, that the great mistake was made by the Court in announcing any decision on this grave constitutional issue without first securing the fully considered concurrence of a reasonably assured majority of the whole Court.

NOTES TO CHAPTER IX

1. *Hepburn* v. *Griswold*, 8 Wall. 603; and *Knox* v. *Lee*, 11 Wall. 682, 12 Wall. 457. See also, *Broderick's Executor* v. *Magraw*, 8 Wall. 639; *Latham's and Deming's Appeals*, 9 Wall. 145; and *Deming's Appeal*, 10 Wall. 251.

2. 12 Stat. 345.

3. As to the other four controversies listed above, the first relates to the national policy of the Legal Tender Act and, therefore, does not necessarily turn upon a question of law. The second and sixth concern the justification, on their merits, of the conflicting views as to the constitutionality of the legal tender provisions of the Act of 1862 and of the applications made of them. The *Legal Tender* cases, *supra*, have decided those controversies in favor of the constitutionality of the Act and its application. See also, *Juilliard* v. *Greenman*, 110 U. S. 421, and *Norman* v. *Baltimore & Ohio R. Co.*, 294 U. S. 240. The fourth concerns the claim that President Grant and the Senate "packed" the Court in order to secure a reversal of the decision of February 7, 1870, *Hepburn* v. *Griswold*, *supra*. In fact, the nominations of Justices Strong and Bradley reached the Senate practically simultaneously with the announcement of that decision, and their propriety now has been well established. "There was no ground for attacking the honesty of the judges or for the suggestion that President Grant had attempted to pack the Court." Hughes, The Supreme Court of the United States (1928), 52. See also, Henry Adams, Historical Essays (1891), 279-317, 392-401; George F. Hoar, The Charge of Packing the Court Against President Grant and Attorney General [E. R.] Hoar Refuted (1896); Charles Bradley, Miscellaneous Writings of the Late Hon. Joseph P. Bradley (1901), 45-74; II Boutwell, Reminiscences of Sixty Years in Public Affairs (1902), 207-211; II Warren, The Supreme Court in United States History (rev. ed. 1928), 498-532; Ratner, Was the Supreme Court Packed by President Grant? 50 Pol. Sci. Q. (1935), 343-358; Fairman, Justice Miller and the Supreme Court (1939), 149-178; Fairman, Mr. Justice Bradley's Appointment to the Supreme Court and the Legal Tender Cases, 54 Harv. L. Rev. (1941), 977-1034, 1128-1155.

4. *Ex parte McCardle*, 6 Wall. 318, 7 Wall. 506. See Burton, *Ex parte Milligan* and *Ex parte McCardle*, 41 A. B. A. J. 121.

5. 14 Stat. 209.

6. 16 Stat. 44.

7. For the interview between Lincoln and Chase, see Piatt, Memories of the Men Who Saved the Union (1887), 105-109. See also, Schuckers, The Life and Public Services of Salmon Portland Chase (1874), 236-256.

8. 2 Duv. (Ky.) 20. Justice Miller, in his dissent in *Hepburn* v. *Griswold*, *supra*, later said, "The two houses of Congress, the President who signed the bill, and fifteen State courts, being all but one that has passed upon the question, have expressed their belief in the constitutionality of these laws." 8 Wall., at 638. Such fifteen state court decisions are identified in Fairman, Mr. Justice Miller and the Supreme Court 1862-1890 (1939), 152-153. They include *Shollenberger* v. *Brinton*, 52 Pa. 9, in which Justice Strong, of the Supreme Court of Pennsylvania, in 1866, wrote an opinion sustaining the constitutionality of the Act. In 1871, the same man, as a Justice of the Supreme Court of the United States, was to write the opinion of that Court to the same effect. *Knox* v. *Lee*, 12 Wall. 457, 529.

9. In its December Term, 1863, in *Roosevelt* v. *Meyer*, 1 Wall. 512, the Court, with Justice Nelson dissenting, had held that, although the validity of the Act was attacked in a New York court, the Supreme Court of the United States had no jurisdiction to review the state decision because the attack had resulted in favor of, rather than against, the constitutionality of the Federal Act. This channel of attack was not reopened until, in its December Term, 1871, the Court, in *Trebilcock* v. *Wilson*, 12 Wall. 687, found jurisdiction under a clause of §25 of the Judiciary Act, which permitted review whenever the *construction* of any clause of the Constitution was drawn into question. In its December Term, 1868, in *Lane County* v. *Oregon*, 7 Wall. 71, the Court confined itself to holding that the Act, in making Treasury notes legal tender for the payment of public and private "debts," did not make them such for the payment of taxes imposed by state authority. At the same Term, the Court had held that a mortgage bond calling expressly for payment in gold or silver could not be satisfied by a tender of Treasury notes. *Bronson* v. *Rodes*, 7 Wall. 229. See also, *Butler* v. *Horwitz*, 7 Wall. 258; *Veazie Bank* v. *Fenno*, 8 Wall. 533.

10. Attorney General Hoar was a brother of Senator George Frisbie Hoar, of Massachusetts, and of unquestionable competency and integrity, but he was personally unpopular in the Senate. II Warren, The Supreme Court in United States History (rev. ed. 1928), 501-507.

11. 16 Stat. 45.

12. This subsequently crucial deferment of the effective date of his resignation may have been due largely to his family's desire to spend the winter in Washington and to the fact that the rental of his rooms there did not expire until February. See letter quoted in Fairman, Mr. Justice Bradley's Appointment to the Supreme Court and the Legal Tender Cases, 54 Harv. L. Rev. (1941), 1004 and 1007.

13. 8 Wall. 639.

14. 8 Pet. 118, 122. In the cases there mentioned, two of the Court's seven members had been absent when the cases had been argued. Of the remaining five members, there were not four who concurred in their answers to the constitutional questions at issue.

15. "It is proper to say that Mr. Justice Grier, who was a member of the court when this cause was decided in conference, and when this opinion was directed to be read, stated his judgment to be that the legal tender clause, properly construed, has no application to debts contracted prior to its enactment; but that upon the construction given to the act by the other judges he concurred in the opinion that the clause, so far as it makes United States notes a legal tender for such debts, is not warranted by the Constitution." 8 Wall., at 626. See also, the Chief Justice's further explanation in his dissenting opinion in *Knox* v. *Lee*, 12 Wall. 457, 572.

16. *Latham's and Deming's Appeals*, 9 Wall. 145. Deming later unsuccessfully sought to reinstate his appeal. *Deming's Appeal*, 10 Wall. 251. See also, Fairman, Mr. Justice Miller and the Supreme Court 1862-1890, *supra*, at 170 and note 64.

17. Fairman, Mr. Justice Miller and the Supreme Court 1862-1890, *supra*, at 170-171. The Chief Justice prepared a statement of his side of the controversy and placed it in the files of the Court. Thereupon, on April 30, the five Justices constituting the new majority approved in detail a counter "Statement of Facts" written by Justice Miller. The Chief Justice then withdrew his statement and Justice Miller's was not filed. The Chief Justice's point of view was, however, reflected in Schuckers' account of the *Legal Tender* cases in his contemporary work, The Life and Public Services of Salmon Portland Chase (1874), 258-268. Much later, Justice Miller's statement, released after the death of all participating Justices, was published by Justice Bradley's son in his collection of the Miscellaneous Writings of the Late Hon. Joseph P. Bradley (1901), 61-74.

18. The judgment is to be found in 11 Wall. 682. The full report is in 12 Wall. 457.

19. After expressly overruling *Hepburn* v. *Griswold*, 8 Wall. 603, the Court referred with approval to the practice announced by Chief Justice Marshall in *Briscoe* v. *Bank of Kentucky, supra:*
"That case was decided by a divided court, and by a court having a less number of judges than the law then in existence provided this court shall have. These cases have been heard before a full court, and they have received our most careful consideration. The questions involved are constitutional questions of the most vital importance to the government and to the public at large. We have been in the habit of treating cases involving a consideration of constitutional power differently from those which concern merely private rights [citing *Briscoe* v. *Bank of Kentucky*, 8 Pet. 118]. We are not accustomed to hear them in the absence of a full court, if it can be avoided. Even in cases involving only private rights, if convinced we had made a mistake, we would hear another argument and correct our error. And it is no unprecedented thing in courts of last resort, both in this country and in England, to overrule decisions previously made. We agree this should not be done inconsiderately, but in a case of such far-reaching consequences as the present, thoroughly convinced as we are that Congress has not transgressed its powers, we regard it as our duty so to decide and to affirm both these judgments." 12 Wall. 457, 553-554.

20. *Scott* v. *Sandford,* 19 How. 393.

21. *Pollock* v. *Farmers' Loan & Trust Co.,* 157 U. S. 429.

22. Hughes, The Supreme Court of the United States (1928), 50. For a tabulation of Acts of Congress held unconstitutional in whole or in part by the Supreme Court of the United States, see Constitution of the United States of America, Analysis and Interpretation, S. Doc. No. 170 (82d Cong., 2d Sess.) 1241-1254. For a further analysis of such decisions and for the composition of the Court when each was rendered, see Provisions of Federal Law Held Unconstitutional by the Supreme Court of the United States (1936), prepared by Wilfred C. Gilbert of the Legislative Reference Service, Library of Congress, especially at 141-147.

X

The Independence and Continuity of the Supreme Court of the United States*

RECENTLY, I WAS interested to hear the answers when a European visitor asked a group of Americans why baseball had such a firm hold on the American public. One said it was because of the skill attained by major league players in doing what so many Americans tried to do in their boyhood, another said it was due to the colorful newspaper, radio and television reporting of the major league games, but the third answer interested me most. It emphasized the independent and competent umpiring of the games. There is much to be said for that frequently overlooked factor which is the typically American way of making competition free, fair and interesting. Without the umpiring, major league baseball would be impossible.

Short informal contests are often conducted without umpires but, if there is to be any long, hard, close and determined contest that is not going to end in a fight or a riot, it is a good American custom for the parties to agree upon one or more umpires before they start, then accept the umpires' decisions while the parties devote themselves to the contest. The system does not call for infallibility on the part of the umpires, but it does require that they be independent of the parties, know the rules, and seek to apply them to the best of their ability, fairly, promptly and courteously. The need for this system is as clear in government as it is in sports. In government, the judges are the umpires—the Constitution and the laws are the rule books. This system provides the best solution yet found for making workable a government of

* An earlier version of this paper appeared in 24 Fordham Law Review 169 (Summer, 1955).

laws, not of men. It implements Equal Justice Under Law.

The lack of an independent judiciary in the American Colonies was one of the reasons that led to our Declaration of Independence. In July, 1776, British judges were doing the "umpiring" in the British Colonies in America. Unlike the judges in England, their commissions did not read *"Quamdiu se bene gesserint,"* that is, "during their good behavior."[1] The commissions of the Colonial judges more often read *"durante bene placito,"* that is, "during the good pleasure" of the King. This meant that the tenure of the Colonial judges was insecure, for it depended upon the unpredictable pleasure of the King and his advisers. Accordingly, in the Declaration of Independence, we find among the complaints against King George III that "He has made Judges dependent upon his will alone, for the tenure of their offices, and the amount and payment of their salaries." In common with the French historian and philosopher, Montesquieu, our founding fathers subscribed to the view "that 'there is no liberty, if the power of judging be not separated from the legislative and executive powers.'"[2] Therefore, our Constitutional Convention of 1787 sought, as far as possible, to guarantee the independence of our new federal judiciary.

The first step was a structural separation of the judicial power from the legislative and executive powers. The authors of the Constitution did this by inserting, after Article I, dealing with legislative power, and Article II, dealing with executive power, a separate Article III, dealing with judicial power. Article III stated that "The judicial Power of the United States, shall be vested in one supreme Court, and such inferior Courts as the Congress may from time to time ordain and establish." It left to Congress the determination of the number of Justices constituting the Supreme Court and also the determination of what, if any, lower federal courts should be created. But it did refer to the Supreme Court as "one supreme Court" thereby placing some emphasis upon the

Court sitting as a unit, as it always has done, rather than in sections, divisions or panels.

Next, they provided that the judges, both of the Supreme and lower Courts, "shall hold their Offices during good Behaviour." That secured for the new federal judges a degree of independence corresponding to that which the people of England had won for their judges.

Thirdly, the authors of the Constitution provided that the judges, both of the Supreme and lower Courts "shall, at stated Times, receive for their Services, a Compensation, which shall not be diminished during their Continuance in Office." By thus providing that federal judges could not be starved out of office, the Constitution corrected the second fault complained of in the Declaration of Independence.

There remained the questions of how best to select the judges and how, in case of a serious violation of their public duty, to remove them from office and yet preserve their independence. The problem of appointment was solved by vesting the nomination in the President and making each appointment subject to the advice and consent of the Senate. The Constitution imposed no formal limitations of age, locality, experience or other qualifications. It relied upon the President and the Senate to make the selections and, by the elimination of fixed terms of office, it produced the result that vacancies rest largely in the hands of Providence and occur at unpredictable intervals.

This brings up an issue which has received recent consideration in Congress. That is, the advisability of imposing, by law, uniform qualifications for appointment to the federal judiciary, or at least to the Supreme Court. Laying aside any question of the constitutionality of a limitation placed by Congress upon the future discretion of the Senate to determine each case on its merits, it may be noted that the Senate, by virtue of the present constitutional provision, already has complete authority to impose or omit uniform standards when it confirms or rejects each nomination.

The question of removal from office was the subject of significant debate. Finally, by vote of seven states to one, the Convention declined to insert a provision that the judges "may be removed by the Executive on the application by the Senate and House of Representatives."[3] While that proposal was modeled upon the right of the British Crown to remove judges upon a joint address of the Houses of Parliament, the federal judges of the United States were relieved of even that traditional control of their tenure.

This left the subject of the removal of federal judges to the standard procedure applicable to federal civil officers, namely, "Impeachment [by the House of Representatives] for, and conviction [by the Senate] of, Treason, Bribery, or other high Crimes and Misdemeanors." Art. II, §4. With this went the important provision that "no Person shall be [so] convicted without the Concurrence of two thirds of the Members [of the Senate] present." This procedure has been applied but once to a Justice of the Supreme Court and, in his case, the Senate, disregarding party lines, refused to convict him by the necessary two-thirds vote.

With these safeguards, the nation ventured into the un-explored regions of representative federal government involving undefined divisions of authority between the federal and state jurisdictions, and equally undefined divisions of authority between the legislative, executive and judicial branches of the federal government itself. If successful, this separation of powers gave promise of a new freedom for the individual in the also undefined areas safeguarded for him by the Bill of Rights, as against the oppression of even his own government.

The Old World watched with incredulity. The plan was loaded with uncertainties and other ingredients of internal combustion. The skeptics had not, however, recognized the strength inherent in the new nation's system of independent umpires available to interpret broad principles in the light of specific circumstances, and to decide questions of jurisdiction as fast as they might arise.

The story of what happened is the story of a living Constitution. The product of the minds of George Washington and the other members of the Constitutional Convention was welded together with such expansion joints that it has met every strain to which the hurricanes and tornadoes of political controversy have subjected it.

It is therefore appropriate to recognize the part that the Supreme Court has played in the development of the nation from one of thirteen states and less than 4,000,000 people to one of forty-eight states, two territories, and several insular possessions governing nearly 175,000,000 people. It has served as the ever-present independent umpire. Confined by the Constitution to deciding only actual cases and controversies (Art. III, §2), it has declined to render advisory opinions on hypothetical questions. This self-restraint has helped to sharpen the line between the judicial function of interpreting existing law and the legislative function of determining future public policy. With equal self-restraint, the judiciary has left the enforcement of the law and of its decisions to the executive branch of the government. It has served as the "living voice of the Constitution."[4]

At this point we come to an interesting and little known by-product of the independence of the Supreme Court, that is, its unique continuity. Unlike the two-year life of a Congress, or even the four-year term of a President, the life of the Supreme Court is continuous. The present Congress is the Eighty-fifth Congress but the Court that sits today is technically the same Court that met in 1790. It is the first Court still sitting. It does not adjourn *sine die*. It adjourns to a time and place prescribed by statute or by itself for its next meeting. Its membership changes only by death, resignation or retirement. There have been but ninety-two Justices serve on the Court. The active members of the Court make use of the accumulated experience of their predecessors, while adapting that experience to new conditions. It is true that only the nine active Justices sit on the Bench and hear the arguments in the new cases. However, they also consult their eighty-three predecessors who are ever present "in the books." Together, the ninety-two share in the decision of the issues.

This continuity of service is not limited to the Justices. All who serve the Court tend to dedicate their lives to it. Loyalty and devotion to the Court as an institution are primary characteristics of service to it.

The Reporters of Decisions

There have been but twelve reporters of its decisions. They report the opinions and draft the headnotes which summarize the decisions of the Court. Lawyers know the names of the first seven because the volumes they published are cited by their names—Dallas, Cranch, Wheaton, Peters, Howard, Black and Wallace. They account for ninety volumes. The next 267 volumes are the work of five equally devoted, but less known, members of the staff. They are Otto, Davis, Butler, Knaebel and Wyatt. Each has rendered distinguished, responsible service.

The spirit and continuity of this service is illustrated by the late Clarence E. Bright. He devoted his life to making the initial prints of the opinions. For seventy-five years, Pearson's Printing Office held the contract and for more than fifty years, Clarence Bright supervised the printing. His devotion is reflected in his touching letter of retirement, which follows:

[155]

Mr. Charles E. Cropley,   July 1, 1946.
Clerk, U. S. Supreme Court,
Washington, D. C.

Dear Mr. Cropley:

Advancing years with an unsatisfactory physical condition compels the decision to relinquish the contract for the Court's printing, as of this date.

The Court's best interest would not be served if I should attempt to carry on, only to find myself lacking in the punch and alertness which I have been able to apply during the past 55½ years.

To have served under 5 Chief Justices and 35 Associate Justices covers a lot of territory. It has been a wonderful experience and the fine treatment accorded me by the Justices leaves nothing to be desired. The splendid and helpful co-operation of your office speaks well for your administration.

This is the hardest decision I have ever been called upon to make, but it is the inevitable result of the passing of time.

With best wishes and high personal regards, I remain

Yours very truly,
C. E. Bright.

Today, his work is entrusted to a small devoted staff of men from the Government Printing Office who operate a shop exclusively for this service in the basement of the Court Building.

The Clerks of the Court

There have been but thirteen Clerks of the Court. In the last 131 years there have been but nine—Carroll, Middleton, McKenney, Maher, Stansbury, Cropley, Willey, Fey and Browning. For example, Harold B. Willey began his service as an Assistant Clerk twenty-eight years before he succeeded Cropley in 1952. Cropley, in turn, had begun his service as a Court page forty years before that. Among the treasures in the Clerk's office is a silver urn which was presented to

Mr. Maher when he had completed fifty years with the Court. The helpful courtesy of the Clerk's staff is traditional.

The Marshal

For many years, the Court used the services of the Marshal for the District of Columbia but, since 1867, it has had its own. In those ninety-one years but six men have held the office. The first was Colonel Richard C. Parsons of Cleveland, who resigned after five years when elected to Congress. The second was John G. Nicolay, who resigned after fifteen years to devote himself to preparing the Nicolay and Hay biography of Lincoln. He was followed by Major John M. Wright, Frank Key Green, Thomas E. Waggaman and T. Perry Lippitt. The present Marshal started his service as a clerk-stenographer in 1935 and became Marshal in 1952. His predecessor started as a page boy and served the Court forty years.

The Librarian

Since 1887, the Court has developed an excellent law library. In those seventy-one years, there have been but four Librarians. Henry DeForest Clarke served thirteen years, Frank Key Green about fourteen years, and Oscar DeForest Clarke, son of the first Librarian, thirty-two years. The present Librarian is Miss Helen Newman, who formerly served as Associate Librarian with Oscar Clarke. She has been with the Court since 1942, and has been in full charge of the Library since 1947.

Law Clerks, Secretaries, Guards and Pages

Each Associate Justice is allowed two law clerks, and the Chief Justice three. They are able young lawyers who serve with anonymity, usually for one or two years. Among them have been Dean Acheson, later Secretary of State, and Calvert Magruder, now Chief Judge of the United States Court of Appeals for the First Circuit.

Invaluable auxiliaries of the Justices are their equally unsung secretaries. Their devoted service often extends throughout their respective Justices' connection with the Court.

The guards of the Court serve under the Marshal. They have police jurisdiction within the area of the Court grounds.

There are four Court pages, of high school age, who serve the Justices both in and out of the courtroom.

The Messengers

Each Justice traditionally is allowed the assistance of a personal messenger of his own selection. In them continuity of service has reached its peak. The longest service that has been rendered to the Court is that of Archibald Lewis, a messenger who served it sixty-three years. Today there is in the service of the Court Harold Joice, now in his thirty-ninth year, following in the footsteps of his father, who served the Court forty-eight years, and of his grandfather, who served it thirty years.

The Bar

The continuity of the Court is matched by that of its Bar. From the earliest days, leaders of the American Bar have assisted the Court in solving its greatest problems. Examples of such recent service of more than fifty years before it are George Wharton Pepper, of Pennsylvania, and the late John W. Davis, of New York.

The Court

The Constitution does not prescribe the size of the Court. Congress at first fixed its membership at six, then seven, then nine, then ten. Soon thereafter, it determined that no new members be appointed until the number had fallen to seven. However, when the number was reduced to eight, Congress restored the limit to nine. Six of the nine constitute a quorum. The Chief Justice bears the title of "Chief Justice of the United States" and is appointed to that office as such.

There have been but fourteen Chief Justices—Jay, John Rutledge, Ellsworth, Marshall, Taney, Salmon P. Chase, Waite, Fuller, White, Taft, Hughes, Stone, Vinson and Warren. The Chief Justice presides not only over the Supreme Court but also over the Judicial Conference of the United States. That Conference consists of the Chief Judges of the eleven Federal Circuits and of one District Judge from each Circuit.

A tradition of the Court that was instituted by Chief Justice Fuller has been scrupulously followed ever since. It is that whenever the members of the Court gather either to go on the Bench or into conference, each Justice shakes hands with each of the other eight—making a total of 36 handshakes on each occasion.

The continuity of judicial service also appears from the fact that the service of seven members of the Court spans its life. A visitor to the Court at any time since 1790 would have found there at least one of the following—Cushing, Marshall, Wayne, Field, White, McReynolds or Black.

The record length of judicial service is that of Justice Field —thirty-four years, eight months and twenty-two days. Others who have served over thirty years are Marshall, Harlan, Story, Wayne, McLean, Washington and William Johnson. Justice Holmes served a little less than thirty years.

At all times, the Senior Justice in point of service lends a special continuity to its work. During two-thirds of the life of the Court, some member of it has had over twenty years of personal experience on it. And since the first nine years of its life, the Court always has had someone on it with nine or more years of membership. The Associate Justices sit on the right and left of the Chief Justice, strictly in the order of their seniority, and change seats only as their seniority changes. As a result of this, one man, and only one, has sat in all nine places. This was Chief Justice Stone, who moved by seniority from the junior to the Senior Associate Justiceship and then was appointed Chief Justice.[5]

There has been an informal but traditional recognition of the value of a geographical distribution in the training and perspective of the Court's members. This has appeared in several lines of succession to the Bench. One example is what might be called the New England Chair on the Court. This was first filled by Cushing of Massachusetts. He was succeeded by Story of Massachusetts, Woodbury of New Hampshire, Curtis of Massachusetts, Clifford of Maine, Gray of Massachusetts, Holmes of Massachusetts, Cardozo of New York, and Frankfurter of Massachusetts. The apparent break in continuity through the succession of Cardozo to Holmes was not actually such because, throughout Cardozo's service, Brandeis of Massachusetts was a member of the Court.

Even more significant than the individual continuity of the Court is its group continuity. The longest period during which the Court has remained unchanged is one of twelve years between the early part of President Madison's term and the latter part of Monroe's. There have been ten periods of five or more years without a change, but evidence of the flexibility of the Court's membership appears in the fact that each President who has served four years or more in office has appointed one or more members of the Court.

The most striking example of this group continuity is that which marked the Court over which Chief Justice Marshall presided. During his nearly thirty-four and a half years of service, he served with but fifteen Associate Justices, and seven of these served with him for extended periods. They were—Thompson for about twelve years, Livingston sixteen years, Todd nineteen years, Story twenty-three years, Duvall twenty-three years, Washington twenty-nine years, and William Johnson thirty years. These are the men who, with him, made up the Court which handed down the decisions that have become the foundation of our constitutional law. These Justices not only made those vital decisions, they nurtured and protected them.

Thus, endowed with independence and continuity, the Supreme Court seeks, day by day, to meet its unique responsibility as the keystone that holds in place the members of the governmental arch which the framers of our Constitution designed to sustain a representative federal republic, dedicated to the preservation for the individual of the greatest freedom consistent with like freedom for all.

NOTES TO CHAPTER X

1. 12 and 13 W. III, c. 2 (1700), and see 1 Blackstone Commentaries (Lewis ed. 1902) *267.

2. LXXVIII The Federalist (Macy Co. 1945) 521, quoting from 3 Montesquieu, Spirit of Laws, 181.

3. Documents Illustrative of the Formation of the Union of the American States (1927), 622-623; 2 Farrand, Records of the Federal Courts of 1787 (1911), 428-429. Such a right of removal upon the joint address of the two Houses of the Legislature exists in several States. Carpenter, Judicial Tenure in the United States (1918), 126-135.

4. I Bryce, The American Commonwealth (3d ed. 1908), 272.

5. The Senior Justices have been Jay, Cushing, Samuel Chase, Washington, Marshall, Story, McLean, Wayne, Nelson, Clifford, Miller, Field, Harlan, White, McKenna, Holmes, Van Devanter, McReynolds, Stone and Black.

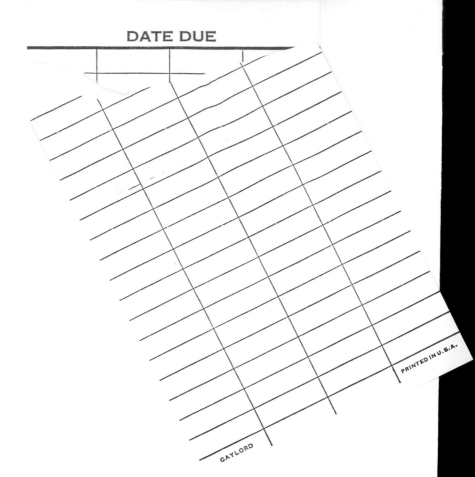

DATE DUE

GAYLORD

PRINTED IN U.S.A.